BRITISH MOTORCYCLES OF THE 1960s

A detailed history
of 50 marques—from
AJS to Wasp

Roy Bacon

First Published in 1988 by Osprey Publishing

This edition Published 1994 by the Promotional
Reprint Co., Ltd exclusively for Bookmart Limited,
Leicester, UK and Treasure Press, Australia

Reprinted 1995

ISBN 1-85648-1662

Printed in China

Half-title page **Excelsior tried this gambit in 1962, when a
few hours' work knocked £40 or so from the machine's
price. The model was the Universal 150, which had an
Excelsior engine, and the pack sold for 99 guineas**

Title page **Vic Willoughby tanking up a 1960 Norton
Dominator 99 de luxe during a road test. Note the pump
in the background still labelled 'POOL', although National
made much play of 'Aromatics' in their product**

Contents

Mike Nicks with a product of the 1960s—a Rickman
Metisse with Triumph engine—THE scrambles tool before
the two-strokes took over

Foreword by Mike Nicks

If all the horror stories spread about British motorcycles were true, the modern phenomenon of a booming classic movement would never have occurred. Nostalgia is an addictive brew, but even the most dedicated enthusiast is unlikely to invest his or her spare time and savings in a motorcycle that is guaranteed to fail at every inconvenient moment.

The reality of the situation is that British bikes were, and are, capable of returning good service if they are ridden and maintained sympathetically in the manner for which they were designed. Remember that for much of the 1960s, most travel was done on sinuous A-roads—much kinder to engines than the high-speed blasts for hours at a time that modern motorcycles are expected to withstand.

Roy Bacon's volumes in the *Osprey Collector's Library* are invaluable for the large amount of information they provide about particular marques or groups of models. If you own a classic British machine, such data is crucial in helping you keep the bike running efficiently, for the traditional dealer in these products has largely disappeared.

But in this book, Roy takes a broad look at the British industry's products over an entire decade. A pretty exciting ten years it was, too, as the British parallel-twin moved toward the epitome of its abilities—in performance terms at least, if not always in reliability or smoothness—and the Japanese invasion took hold. The book provides a roll-call of models for those moving into the classic scene and wondering which bikes to consider. It will also be of service to those many students of motorcycling history who may wish to ponder on the trends and output of the British industry as a whole, rather than just one manufacturer.

Also covered here are the 'little' people—the manufacturers of such brands as DKR, Heldun, Sapphire and Scorpion. Few, if any, of their products survive, but it is fascinating to look back on the efforts of these firms who strove to make a living in one of the most financially hazardous ways known to man—by designing and attempting to sell their own motorcycles!

There were faults with British motorcycles of the 1960s; the author points them out in his introductory chapter. But the best of these machines had a charisma and an appeal—'macho' is the word that people use for this quality nowadays—that are at the very heart of the classic motorcycling movement.

Mike Nicks,
EDITOR
Classic Bike

The machine that changed the motorcycle world and
became the two-wheeled Model T or VW Beetle—the
Honda 50, of which many millions were sold worldwide.
This is a 1959 Super Cub

The pendulum swings

The British motorcycle industry entered the 1960s on an all-time high, and few could have foreseen how things would change by 1970. Trade was at its most buoyant at the beginning of the decade, and firms that had come through the depression, the war and post-war austerity had seen the boom years of the 1950s culminate in their best year ever in 1959. Sales for that 12-month period had reached a record 331,806 units, but sadly this figure would not be reached again.

That year was exceptional for a number of reasons. Among them was the weather, which remained dry and warm from March to October, setting new records for the century. Under such balmy skies, more new riders were ready to take to two wheels, for the perils of rain and dark nights were never part of the salesman's patter.

Then there were social changes. After the war, many new housing estates had been built, and most were on the outskirts of towns and cities. In addition, many industries had moved to new factories which, invariably, were located away from housing within easy reach of major roads, the rail network, airports and even canals. Offices were frequently rebuilt on their original inner-city sites, but with many more storeys and far more occupants. Few had adequate parking arrangements. Other companies moved from the towns to new rural sites, and their employees had the same travel problems as the factory workers.

Thanks to these changes, the factory worker found his journey to work growing much longer, while his office counterpart faced densely-packed public transport as more people sought to reach the large office blocks at the same time. It was a drastic change from the era when most walked or cycled to work because it was so close to home.

For many, some form of personal transport became essential, as often the new housing estates lacked a bus service and were far from any railway. The bicycle played its part but fell from favour as journeys lengthened, money became more plentiful and riders became older or took more responsible positions. Owning a car was the aim of all, but aside from the expense, was not always a complete solution to the problems of the husband's need to get to work and the wife's need to go shopping, get to schools and maybe a part-time job.

The office worker was more inclined to want four wheels but had more problems with them. Far fewer towns and cities had adequate bypasses at that time, so traffic snarl-ups and parking problems were major difficulties.

It was also a time of full employment, reasonable wages, security, little or no inflation and shorter working hours. During the 1950s there had been credit squeezes, petrol rationing in 1956 due to the Suez crisis, and variations in the rate of purchase tax (eventually replaced by VAT).

Late in 1958, many of the controls were relaxed or removed, setting the stage for a boom in 1959 (which just happened to be an election year). This was the final incentive, and that season people bought mopeds, scooters and motorcycles in large numbers to get to work on (beating the traffic jams and parking problems) and for leisure use.

Thus, 1959 was the peak year for sales of new machines, but it was not all good news for the home industry. About half of the machines sold here were imported models—mainly mopeds and scooters. These may have occupied the low-value end of the market, but this was an area of expansion where the British industry had few pickings.

In fact, many of the buyers of these machines were in no way motorcycle customers. They might have begun with a moped, but this would simply have been a means of getting to work cheaply and quickly. From the moped, they might have graduated to a scooter, but often moved straight to a small car as soon as their finances allowed.

Scooter customers bought for similar reasons in many cases, but with the added bonus of an active social scene to attract them. The Lambretta and Vespa importers realized how important this was and were quick to become involved in fostering the social-club image. The motorcycle clubs, on the other hand, were run by enthusiasts with limited interest from the manufacturers.

There were two more events that were to play a major part in the changes to come in the 1960s. The first was the launch of the Mini in 1959. At a stroke, it killed off the majority of bubble-cars and three-wheelers, most of which were pretty dreadful. At £500, the Mini offered a four-seat saloon car with incredibly good road-holding that was fun to drive. Its appearance also dealt a major blow to the traditional sidecar market, which began to shrink and concentrate on a smaller number of very sporting outfits. There were still some sales of scooters with sidecars attached, but these were not in the same class and so were less affected by the Mini.

The second event occurred halfway round the world in Japan. Few in Europe had any knowledge of that country and its motorcycle industry, which had existed behind high tariff barriers during the 1950s. Its history stretched back to Edwardian times, but even in the 1920s, when there was something of a boom, the number of machines was very small, for boats and animals were the means of transport used by the masses.

In those days most motorcycles in Japan were imported from Europe or the USA, but the numbers were restricted to protect the Japanese industry. Although this continued, military expansion dictated a need for far more home-grown transportation. Then, in the 1930s, came a deal with Harley-Davidson who sold the Japanese the rights to an old design and helped them perfect mass-production, quality-control and the necessary metal-treatment techniques. This was all new in Japan, and the motorcycle factory that came about from the deal became the focal point for this knowledge. It was visited by many Japanese engineers from all manner of industries. As a result, Japanese working practice was hurled forward to modern times, although motorcycle output remained minimal, with 1940 being the peak year when about 3000 machines were produced.

Post-war Japan was desperate for transport of any form, and this led to a mass of small motorcycle firms building all manner of machines,

most of them crude and only just better than walking. By the beginning of the 1950s, there were over 100 motorcycle firms, although total production for 1950 was still only 2633.

Over the next decade, this situation changed completely. The number of firms shrank rapidly in a ruthless sales war, while production rose at an enormous rate. British and European designs were copied at first, but the intense competition acted as a forcing house for Japanese designers. Many found themselves moving from firm to firm as some collapsed and others were taken over, but every time this happened they learnt something new and they took the best they had found with them.

During this time, the world at large was ignored. Massive tariff barriers were used to keep out foreign imports, and from 1955 currency regulations made it impossible for a private citizen to buy anything other than a Japanese machine. These restrictions were waived for the manufacturers who were encouraged to import samples from all over the world to study and copy.

By the end of the decade they had saturated their own docile home market, and in 1959 production had reached three-quarters of a million machines, far more than any other country, but outside Japan they were unknown.

With the home market full, they had to look further afield, and so began the great Japanese export drive. America and Europe were the targets, and Honda spearheaded the attack by selling motorcycling in general to the public at large outside the usual markets. This was good for the industry as a whole, but virtually all the sales were of small-capacity machines, and these were seldom of British manufacture.

In 1958 Honda had launched the C100 Super Cub scooterette which finally fulfilled the 'everyman' dream of all makers. For years it was believed that the right formula would release untapped markets to the motorcycle industry, and many firms had gone down seeking this Eldorado.

Pre-war attempts had failed because the machines were too slow or too heavy, while post-war the moped and scooter were potential solutions. The former had too limited a performance in its early forms, but the latter came close to the answer. It worked well enough in developed countries with paved roads, but elsewhere it was less successful. The small wheels inherent in the design made for difficult handling on dirt roads, and the machines were not quite what was

Scooters were an important part of the scene in 1960 and
had a strong social aspect. This is the Isle of Man rally
that year, the competitors turning up Summer Hill
with Douglas seafront and horse tram behind them

needed in poorer countries. The Velocette LE overcame the handling difficulties, but there were other problems that prevented it being produced in great numbers.

The Honda scooterette changed all this and went on to be made in millions. It sold worldwide and introduced two-wheel travel, on well-made but inexpensive products, to many. By the mid-1960s, Honda was to motorcycling what Hoover was to vacuum cleaners.

Back in Britain, the motorcycle industry told themselves that this was a passing phase and were certain that the Japanese would never make big motorcycles. This head-in-the-sand attitude prevailed, despite the further increase in Japanese production levels to over two million units a year and the appearance of small Honda motorcycles on British roads.

These early machines might have been only of 125 or 250 cc, but they offered a level of performance and degree of sophistication that domestic manufacturers could not match. They were backed by an exciting road-racing programme that quickly dominated most of the world's classic events, and this was coupled with some heavy advertising in traditional and new areas.

The British scene was already under pressure, for the rise in sales and considerable increase in new riders during 1959 had brought about a corresponding rise in accident levels. Around the same time the cults of mods and rockers (the former on scooters and the latter on fast motorcycles) gained wide followings, and the media were handed some juicy stories.

There were invasions of seaside towns, gang fights and bypass burn-ups. Allied to this was the general dislike of the noise, whether the high-pitched note of the mod scooter with its altered silencer or the thunder of a Gold Star on full rattle—motorcycling had a bad name.

One change came quickly and took the form of an act to restrict learner riders to 250 cc machines. Prior to that, a 16-year-old could straddle a hot 650 and hammer up the new M1 for 60-odd miles with neither speed limit nor helmet to hinder him. The new law came into force in 1961 but did not have quite the effect expected, as the politicians and bureaucrats failed to consider all the effects, as usual.

The first point they missed was that the change in the law had virtually no effect on scooter riders, as very few of these bought machines over 250 cc

anyway. Those who did tended to be more experienced riders who did not have accidents or cause trouble. Next was a clause that allowed the learner to ride a machine of any capacity if it was hitched to a sidecar. Quickly the young twigged that the way to go was a 650 with a chair, which you sold to the next learner as soon as you had passed your test, leaving you with the 650 you wanted in the first place. Thus, many riders had their first solo experience on a big twin, and the sidecar miles were of little help.

The machines themselves began to reflect the capacity limit, and soon the plodding 250 cc models of the late 1950s were joined by sports versions. Often, the extra power came from measures which made the machines harder to ride and, therefore, less suitable for a learner to start on. Frequently, manufacturers would list a hot 250 and cooking 350 of similar performance, and it was the latter which would have been better for the learner.

The final aspect of this capacity limit was on the sales of British machines. Novices found themselves in the showroom confronted by the sophisticated Honda 250 with its very high performance and full range of equipment. They compared this with what the British industry offered and, more often than not, the outcome was another Honda sale. The fact that the British machine handled better was not known by a newcomer, and few could have exploited this anyway. What they wanted to do was blast down the bypass faster than the other learners and, in most cases, the Honda did just that.

Thus, the British industry began to give up the small-bike end of the market. They thought that there was not enough profit in it and that they could concentrate on the 500 cc-plus market, once Honda had kindly got the customers started on two wheels. Of course, many merely rode their Hondas for a while and then moved on to cars, but some did continue with big BSAs, Nortons or Triumphs. Often, they would compare their new large model with the old small machine and frequently this reinforced their brand loyalty to Honda.

At the end of the 1950s, the larger, and a few smaller, British machines had been aimed at achieving a cleaner and better image for motorcycling, with more enclosure and a better range of screens and fairings. This did not last, and the cult of the café racer soon came into being, running alongside the enthusiast at the local club, the commuter and the scooterist.

The clubmen tended to despise café racers, and the term originated as a derogatory reference to riders who only rode from café to café and covered no great distance. For some this was true, but others rode to race meetings on most weekends and in this way covered quite a large annual mileage. The trade liked them, for they bought expensive models, added pricey extras and would pay for good service. As a bonus, they kept their machines spotless, so that giving them a service was a pleasure compared with some more traditional customers who brought in engines caked with grease and mud.

The beginning of the end for the British industry occurred in 1965 when Honda announced the CB450. This offered performance with an engine that had not one but two overhead-camshafts allied to valves held shut by torsion-bar springs. The Japanese had moved into the 500 cc class, and the protective bubble the British firms had enjoyed burst.

There was some response in the form of bigger engines and a little restyling, but in most cases the machines showed their elderly roots all too plainly. Furthermore, the passage of the 1960s had brought about an expansion of the motorway system and a considerable increase in dual-carriageways and town bypasses.

The road improvements made it possible to ride much further and faster than before. A run up the A1 from London had involved trickling through many towns on the way north, but this was no longer the case. Bypasses allowed machines to run at speed for much longer periods.

So travel began to take on a new and faster style, demanding more from engines. The Japanese continued to meet this demand, and their greatest blow to the competition came in 1968 with the CB750 Honda. This offered four cylinders, a single overhead-camshaft, disc front brake and five-speed gearbox. It was a sophisticated package at a reasonable price, and it was readily available.

In the previous year, Suzuki had followed their excellent and popular 250 cc Super Six model with the T500. This was a 500 cc, twin-cylinder two-stroke that was fast and bulletproof. In 1968, the range of larger Japanese models was joined by the Kawasaki H1 with its three-cylinder two-stroke engine and outrageous performance, thirst and handling.

None of these machines handled as well as the best European models, but they were adequate, well styled, very well made and available. They sold well, and the British industry had to fight a rearguard action to preserve what it could. This spilled over into the 1970s and at times involved politics and the government of the day, but by then the Japanese were building millions of machines and dominating the scene.

It was a sad end for many British firms which had kept going through some difficult times, but they had made their choice in the early 1950s when they kept to their existing models and failed to invest in the future. It took a decade or more for this short-sightedness to catch up with them, but in the end time ran out.

What was left of the industry concentrated on what it did best—one-offs, small-batch production, specials in café racer or custom form, competition machines and chassis that handled really well. It was to take Japan another decade to catch up in that last elusive and often empirical subject. Until then, frames from the specialists became much sought after, while the 1970s saw another boom in motorcycles, thanks to ever increasing congestion and the rapid rise of oil prices world-wide.

It lasted through the decade, but never again did UK sales reach the 1959 total. The nearest they came was in 1980, but then the figures dropped once more and motorcycling turned to a classic revival. This grew through the 1980s, and the British motorcycles of the 1950s and 1960s were in demand once more—the Triton cult was revived again. British motorcycles became classics world-wide, and many went to collectors in Japan, taking the wheel full circle.

AJS & Matchless

Both AJS and Matchless have been considered together, as in most cases, the models in one range had their exact counterparts in the other. Therefore, the model numbers only are given in alphabetical order without the marque, unless this is needed for clarity. The early post-war distinction of magneto position on the heavyweight singles had long gone by the 1960s, tank badge, timing case and transfers being the only variation. Because of this, it is said that when machines were hauled up on to the factory roof for the annual publicity photos, only one of each type was taken. With it went the appropriate parts for a quick transformation from one marque to the other.

AMC produced quite an extensive range in 1960, with a dozen road and competition models, plus one racing single, under each marque. That year the road models had a new duplex frame, the scramblers were improved and the twins fitted with a nodular iron crankshaft to overcome breakage problems.

Bottom of the range were the 14 and G2 models, which dated from mid-1958 and provided the firm with a 248 cc machine to offer against other small four-strokes. They were often known as the 'lightweights', but at 325 lb this was something of a misnomer and became simply a means of distinguishing them from the traditional singles, which became the 'heavyweights'.

The 250 engine used AMC's existing design of overhead valves, hairpin springs and oil pump. However, it differed in that the cylinder head was swung round so that the inlet and exhaust lay at an angle to the fore-and-aft line. This allowed the use of a short camshaft (gear driven from the crank) with followers and pushrods set to the right rear of the cylinder. The points were at the end of the camshaft and an alternator to the left of the crank.

What made the engine unusual was that, although it looked to be of unit construction, incorporating the gearbox, the latter was in a separate shell. This was drum shaped and could be rotated to set the primary-chain tension. The drawback was that it needed three pints of oil, as a mere two would not wet the gear teeth, and many wore out prematurely because of this.

Another unusual feature was dry-sump lubrication, the oil being held in a chamber formed within the timing cover. This removed the need for external oil pipes and made for a neat engine unit. It went into a composite frame formed from both tubes and pressings. Telescopic front forks and rear pivoted fork provided the suspension, while the wheels had full-width hubs and drum brakes.

The basic road model was soon joined by the 14CS and G2CS scrambles versions, which had tuned engines, strengthened frames, bigger wheels, alloy guards and open exhausts. As these turned the scales at 90 lb more than a Greeves and cost an extra £10 as well, they found few takers.

More successful were the 8 and G5 models, which appeared for 1960 and were 348 cc versions of the smaller lightweight, having much in common. The cylinder was longer, making the engine taller, while the front forks were the Teledraulics used on heavier models.

Alongside these new singles ran the older types which had their roots in the 1930s. By 1960, the road machines had lost their magneto and dynamo, which had a major effect on the appearance of the right side, but a magneto continued for competition use.

The singles came in 348 and 497 cc sizes and were firmly set in the traditional mould of the British single. The crankcase was split vertically and the four-speed gearbox was a separate assembly driven by a chain on the left with the

The so-called AMC light single that appeared to be of unit construction, but was rooted in the past

Above **Trio of Matchless G50 road racers lined up in 1959 for dispatch, and typical of a type that was to revive classic racing two decades later**

Above right **The AJS equivalent of the G50 was the smaller 7R, which shared cycle parts. This is a 1960 model**

Right **The very traditional AJS road single, as sold in 1961. By then, it had gained coil ignition and a duplex frame, but otherwise it was still much as in pre-war days**

Right **The AMC single style from 1964 included Norton forks and hubs, the model also being badged as an ES2**

final-drive on the same side. The frames had duplex down-tubes for road use, but the competition models retained a single tube; all had telescopic forks and pivoted-fork rear suspension.

The 497 cc scrambles models had the oil tank moved to the left side for 1960, leaving room for a GP carburettor and an air filter. They were also available in road trim, and in this form had an alternator and a battery tucked in under the air filter.

The road models were listed in the two engine sizes as the 348 cc 16 and G3, and the 497 cc 18 and G80. The competition machines were the 16C and G3C, which were produced for trials use, and the 18CS and G80CS, which were scramblers. Neither small scrambler nor large trials model were listed.

The rest of the road range comprised the 498 and 646 cc twin-cylinder models. Only one of the former was listed as the model 20 or G9 standard, and these were much as the original 1948 models. They were unique among their contemporaries in having a centre main bearing for the crankshaft, but the separate cylinders and heads made for an engine assembly that was not as rigid as it might

Above left **The scrambles version of the 'light' AMC single, as seen in 1961, when battery ignition replaced the troublesome energy-transfer system**

Left **The AJS model 18, or Statesman as it was known in 1962, when on this road test. A traditional machine, but out-dated, despite an option of an overall blue finish with white mudguards**

have been. As a result, the stiff, one-piece crankshaft was often at odds with its case and bearings, inhibiting performance.

In other respects the twin engine followed conventional lines, having gear-driven camshafts high up in the crankcase to the front and rear of the cylinders. By 1960, there was an alternator on the left end of the crank and a distributor in the old magneto position behind the engine, but this only applied to the 498 cc and standard 646 cc models. The de luxe and CSR versions of the latter retained the separate magneto and dynamo, this last being strapped to the front of the crankcase where it was gear driven. The CS was the same when fitted with the optional lighting set, but normally came with magneto only.

The standard and de luxe models differed only cosmetically, and what was stock on the de luxe was offered as an option on the standard machine. The more sporting models were listed as the 31CS and G12CS, and the 31CSR and G12CSR. All these had the scrambles frame, and the CS versions were built as sports scramblers with siamezed pipes, alloy mudguards, off-road tyres, a small petrol tank and a competition dualseat. The lights, if fitted, were quickly detachable.

The CSR models were built as fast road machines and retained the standard tank and tyres but had an engine with raised compression ratio. The frame, mudguards and exhaust pipes were the same as the CS.

Finally, there were the two road-racing singles, which were very similar and listed as the 349 cc

AJS 7R and the 496 cc Matchless G50. Both had a single-cylinder engine, with chain-driven, single overhead-camshaft, based on a design first seen in 1948 and derived from a pre-war AJS.

By 1960, the machines were reaching the end of their development but had various detail improvements for the season. Among these were frame changes to improve clearance, but in general the machines continued as they were with separate four-speed gearbox, duplex cradle frame, massive conical hubs and large fuel tank.

With one exception, the entire range continued for 1961, the odd man out being the 31CS and G12CS model. However, the same number of machines was offered with the addition of the 248 cc 14S and G2S model. This had more chrome and semi-drop bars, while the engine was made to produce more power by fitting the CS model camshaft.

The scrambles 250 was given coil ignition for 1961, which got rid of the embarrassing energy-transfer system, but the rest of the singles saw little change. This applied to the twins as well, and even the racing singles were altered in detail only.

The end of the year brought changes for the 1962 range, the 498 cc twin being dropped together with the 646 cc de luxe model to leave only two versions of the larger machine in each

Above **Impressive G12 Majestic in 1963 form, on show at Earls Court minus a stolen kneegrip rubber**

Right **Joe Dunphy, during the 1963 Thruxton 500-mile race, on a year-old G12CSR with the seldom-seen rev-counter drive**

make. The CSR models were given the road frame but otherwise were altered little. At the other end of the capacity scale, the three 250s continued, as did the lightweight 350, although this last was dropped in July 1962.

The 497 cc heavyweights continued as they were, as did the trials 348 cc machine, but the smaller road models were replaced by standard and sports machines with a shorter-stroke engine which had pushrod tunnels in the cylinder.

For 1962, all models had a name as well as a number, but this had little effect on the buying public or the trade who continued to refer to them as the model 18, G3 and so on. There was also a new, larger twin listed as the Matchless G15 or G15/45. This had a 750 cc engine, and 195 of them were made that year in two batches. Some details and the finish varied between these, so their appearance could be similar to standard or CSR-specification twins.

Unlike later large twins, the 1962 model was based on the AMC design but with bigger cylinders and a crankcase modified to suit them. Many parts were common to the 646 cc engine, as was most of the cycle side. Cycle parts came from various versions, so the result was unique and striking in the CSR style.

The two racing singles continued with a few more changes to wring the last ounce of performance from them. They were joined by a road version of the larger machine, which was listed as the Matchless G50CSR. The idea was to build 25 so they could run in the 200-mile race at Daytona, and for this they needed lights and a generator. This was achieved by fitting the engine into a CSR frame, clamping a belt-driven dynamo to the front of the crankcase and listing the racing carburettor and megaphone as options.

In May 1962, one further model was added to the list as the 14CSR or G2CSR. This was a super sports version of the basic 240 cc model with tuned engine, full-width hubs, front air scoop, heavy-duty forks from the scrambler and a brighter finish. It ran on in this form for 1963

together with the basic model, but both the CS and S versions were dropped. Also cut was the sports version of the 348 cc heavyweight, but the basic model continued, as did the trials version and the road and scrambles machines with the 497 cc single-cylinder engine.

The 646 cc twin continued with a new front hub, which had appeared on the G15 the year before and also equipped the larger 1963 singles. There were other detail alterations, but only the standard and CSR twins were listed. A few racing singles were built, but early in the year AMC decided to halt production of these models, bringing an era to an end.

The range contracted further for 1964 and, at the same time, the effects of amalgamating Norton production with the AMC line at Plumstead began to take effect. All the road models were fitted with Norton forks and hubs, changing their appearance.

The basic models 11 and G2 were dropped, but the CSR versions continued. All the other singles joined the big scrambler in its length of stroke, so all had integral pushrod tubes which had a further

Matchless G80CS with lights and battery added for road, trail or enduro use

effect on their looks. They were fitted with the Norton oil pump, thus losing another familiar AMC feature. There were still four models listed under each marque, with 348 and 497 cc road, 348 cc trials and 497 cc scrambles machines to be had. The twins carried on, and all went to 12-volt electrics, while there were other changes for the CSR alone.

In 1965 the range ran on minus the 348 cc trials model but with the addition of some larger twins. These were the standard 33 and G15 models, and the sports 33CSR and G15CSR. All had the 745 cc Norton Atlas engine, Norton forks and wheels, so only the frame, tank and accessories remained AMC parts. The CSR models had a very nice line with swept-back exhaust pipes, low bars, rearsets and gaitered front forks.

The days of the true AMC models were fast nearing their end, and there was little change for 1966. The one real alteration that year was to the scrambler, which was only built as the Matchless G85CS. In this form, it had a duplex frame, machined AMC front hub, 7R rear hub and a central oil tank.

The 248 cc model had a semi-sweptback exhaust pipe for 1966, but during that year this machine, together with the 348 and 497 cc singles and the two 646 cc twins were all dropped from the AJS range.

In September 1966, the company was taken over by Manganese Bronze and renamed Norton-Matchless. It continued to produce the scrambler in small numbers right through to 1969, and the 745 cc AJS twins during 1967. The Matchless twins were joined by the G15CS early that year, and this machine followed the line of the earlier CS model with a small tank, trail tyres and capacitor ignition.

For 1968 the standard twin became the G15 Mk2 with the same form of ignition, which was also fitted to the CSR models. In these forms, the three twins and the scrambles single ran on into 1969 when production ceased.

The old factory closed for good in 1971 and was later demolished, but although the Matchless name was no more, until revived in 1987 with a foreign engine, the AJS marque was to live on. This was on a range of two-strokes which are described in the following chapter.

AJS two-strokes

When the traditional AJS models went out of production, the name remained with the Norton Villiers (later NVT) group and was revived in 1967 for a small road-racing model. This came about because Villiers staff member Peter Inchley had taken a fine third place in the 1966 TT riding a special with a Villiers engine. For 1967 the machine became an AJS using the same engine in a new frame, but unfortunately he had to retire from the TT that year through no fault of his own.

From this work came two models late in 1967, both with 247 cc Villiers Starmaker engines. The first was the Double T Racer with six-speed gearbox and twin fuel tanks, one normal and the other under the seat. Soon after its introduction, the machine was named the AJS Starmaker.

The second model was the Alamos scrambler with a lower degree of engine tune, four-speed gearbox and cycle parts to suit. Neither model really got off the ground, although the works machines produced good results during 1968. The group then decided that off-road was the way to go, so the road racer was dropped.

For 1969 the Alamos was replaced by the Y4 scrambler, which had the same engine but revised cycle parts. It was joined by the 37A-T 246 cc trials model, which was similar but shorter, having a single down-tube in place of the two on the scrambler. There were other differences too, the scrambler using AJS forks and 5 in. diameter brakes, while the trials bike had Metal Profiles forks and 6 in. brakes.

At the end of 1969, the trials model was dropped, but the Y4 continued in Mk2 form and was joined by an enlarged 368 cc Y5 version. For

The 1967 AJS Double T Racer with Villiers Starmaker engine and twin fuel tanks

1970 only, both were accompanied by similar models listed as the Y40 and Y50, both being designed for sale in the USA.

The two scramblers continued into the 1970s but were swept into a backwater by the major trials and tribulations experienced by the industry. They might have sunk without a trace, but in time the name and range were bought by Fluff Brown who continued to produce them under the FB-AJS label.

A 1968 two-stroke AJS in ISDT form with road-legal equipment and aids to repair

Right **An AJW Fox Cub with 48 cc Minarelli engine and three speeds, on test late in 1960**

AJW

AJW was a small firm that kept going when many others fell by the wayside; the company's name came from its founder, Arthur John Wheaton. It began producing machines in the late 1920s, kept going through the depressed 1930s and made a further appearance after World War 2.

Production lapsed at the end of 1951, but the marque was revived in 1958 with a light motorcycle. This was the Fox Cub, which was powered by a 48 cc Italian Minarelli two-stroke engine of unit construction with three speeds. The engine was fitted in a spine frame with telescopic front and pivoted-fork rear suspension, 23 in. wheels, full-width hubs and 4 in. brakes. This smart model had light-alloy hubs for 1959. It was joined by two more machines for 1961, one of which was the Vixen with a tuned engine installed in a duplex frame with hydraulic damping for the forks and a larger fuel tank. The other was a moped named the Giulietta. At first, it came with a saddle, but from the middle of the year a dualseat was fitted.

These models had minor changes for 1962, when they were joined by the 49.7 cc Giulietta Super Sport, built in a similar manner to the Vixen as a light motorcycle. It was joined by a four-speed version for 1964, while the other models continued with minor alterations.

The marque faded from the scene at the middle of the decade, but continued to exist and returned to the marketplace around 1974.

Alta Suzuki

The Alta Suzuki was a miniature trials machine developed by Peter Gaunt after he had left the Royal Enfield works team. He joined Suzuki GB when that company was part of the AMC group and, at first, rode a modified 250 cc twin or a B100P lightweight. Once Suzuki were on their own, Gaunt continued this theme with some success, using a bored-out 128 cc machine, and in 1969 he began to build replicas. A little later, Suzuki changed direction to link with Alta while retaining Gaunt as a rider, but he soon left to follow his own star.

At that point, the Alta was still a modified Suzuki, but a few months later a new machine appeared that was strikingly different. It had the Suzuki B105P engine, bored out to 118 cc and fitted with a dual-ratio arrangement to double up on the three standard gears. This unit went into a monocoque frame constructed of light-alloy sheet, riveted together, so it was a true lightweight. However, the new frame failed to find favour with the buying public, so it was changed for a tubular one during 1970 and shed a few more pounds in the process.

Late that year, the price of the engine unit to Alta rose significantly, so they decided to stop production rather than have too expensive a model on the market.

The short-lived Alta Suzuki, seen here in the 1970 Scottish Six Days Trial ridden by Martin Lampkin

Ambassador

By the 1960s, the once extensive range of the Ascot-based Ambassador firm had shrunk to just three models. These were supplemented by the German Zundapp range of mopeds, motorcycles and scooters which combined to give the firm adequate coverage of the small-capacity market.

Of the home-brewed models, the smallest was the Popular, which had the 174 cc Villiers 2L engine with a three-speed gearbox. It was also available with four speeds, and in both forms had a loop frame with telescopic forks and pivoted-fork rear suspension.

Next came the 3 Star Special, which was fitted with the 197 cc Villiers 9E engine and, again, was listed with a three- or four-speed gearbox. While the frame and suspension were similar to the smaller model, its appearance differed considerably. Most noticeable was the front mudguard, which was deeply valanced and had side panels extending to the hub along the line of the forks. The rear of the machine was also enclosed, leaving just the hub in view, while a further steel pressing went over the handlebars to conceal the control cables.

Line of models outside Comerfords' showrooms at Thames Ditton late in 1959, with a Super S Ambassador to the fore

Left **The Ambassador Sports Super S with tuned (so they said) Villiers 2T engine and café-racer style**

Right **Ambassador Popular with 9E engine, outside the Ascot factory in 1962**

Earlier Ambassador Popular, with smaller 2L engine, which was built up to 1960

Twin horns were fitted, one on each side of the rear enclosure, and the seat lifted off to give access to the battery and tools. The name of the machine was shown in the form of three 'star' pressings attached to each side of the rear enclosure. To assist in keeping its rider clean, it had a fully-enclosed rear chain.

The final model was the Super S, which had the 249 cc Villiers 2T twin-cylinder engine, and the 3 Star cycle parts. The side motif was altered to suit, and this larger model had 7 in. brakes in place of the 6 in. versions on the 3 Star, although the hubs of both were of the full-width type.

The Popular was dropped at the end of the year, but other models appeared to enlarge the range. First of these was the Electra 75, which was based on the Super S but had a Siba Dynastart unit on the right-hand side of its crankshaft to provide electric starting. A 12-volt electric system was used, and the ignition and starter key went into a switch set in the right-hand engine cover.

Ambassador and Villiers had enough confidence in the system to dispense with the kickstarter, and no emergency circuit was provided as the machine could be push-started easily, even if the battery was flat. The engine had a raised compression ratio and larger carburettor to improve its output so that it could overcome the extra drag of the Siba when it was acting as a generator.

The rest of the machine was as the Super S, with a new side flash for the name. Various improvements were made in 1961. These were mainly details but did include a revised tank style and a new headlamp mounting which dispensed with the fork brackets used previously.

The Electra 75 stood out from the Super S thanks to a gold and black finish and whitewall tyres. The other twin and the 3 Star Special continued much as before, but in the new year were joined by a Sports Super S, which had the tuned 2T engine and café racer styling. This took the form of dropped bars, flyscreen, small mudguards and less extensive rear enclosure.

Before the introduction of the Sports Super S, however, the firm sprang a surprise by announcing a scooter, which was simply listed as the Ambassador. It had the 174 cc Villiers 3L engine with four-speed gearbox which, though similar to the unit fitted to the older Popular, was fan cooled and incorporated a Siba Dynastart.

The scooter's main frame was a tube with cross-members and a subframe at the rear to support the engine and the seat. At the rear was a pivoted fork which carried the wheel and was controlled by a spring on each side with one damper fitted on the right. At the front was a leading-link fork with the pivot behind the wheel. This was controlled by a single spring-and-damper unit attached to the right leg.

The mechanics were enclosed by bodywork, access being through two side panels or from under the seat. The weathershield swept up to a panel for the speedometer, switches and warning lights, which included one for low fuel level. The tank itself went under the seat and had a rear-mounted filler. A massive front mudguard turned with the forks, but was sprung so it had to be deep to allow for wheel movement. It gave a rather heavy appearance to the scooter's front end. The wheels had full disc rims of 12 in. diameter, and each was held by three fixings. Brakes were 6 in., the pedal for the rear one being matched by a rocking pedal for the gear-change.

For 1962 the five existing models continued unchanged and were joined by two more. One revived the Popular name but was fitted with a 197 cc Villiers 9E engine and three-speed gearbox. It used many parts from the 3 Star model but had a less ambitious, although still well-valanced, front mudguard. The rear enclosure was also cut down to a skirt and a rear mudguard was fitted. Economies were made by fitting 5 in. brakes in offset hubs and direct lighting. It sold at a budget price.

The second new model was a moped with a 49.9 cc Villiers K engine and two-speed gearbox. This was hung from a pressed-steel spine frame with rear suspension and short leading-link forks. Styling was neat and of the period.

All this activity and new models with their associated expensive tooling proved to be very costly, and it was not reflected by any great increase in sales, for the general trend in these was down rather than up. The result was a financial crisis which came to a head in October 1962 when the manufacturing rights were sold to DMW, who moved the operation to their Dudley works. The scooter, moped and Popular disappeared, but the rest of the range continued with some DMW influence on them. The Sports Super S became the Sports Twin but was soon dropped.

During 1963, both ranges were revamped and appeared again with common basic parts and different styling and badges. Thus, the Ambassador models had frames with a main loop formed from square-section tubing (as was DMW practice), while the rear enclosure material was changed to fibreglass.

Three models were listed—the 3 Star Special, Super S and Electra 75—the twins being fitted with Villiers 4T engines for 1964. However, this was to be their last year, for DMW brought the line to a halt and continued with their own marque alone.

The Ambassador scooter, which had the electric-start 3L model of the 174 cc Villiers engine, but did nothing to help the firm's finances

Ariel

To most enthusiasts of the marque, Ariel ceased to be of interest in the 1960s, for they brought production of their four-stroke models to a halt late in 1959. This left them with the enclosed Leader model, which was a far cry from the sturdy Hunters and unique Square Four of earlier years and which appealed to a different type of rider altogether.

One export model did survive as the 650 Cyclone twin for the US market, but only for 1960. It had what was really a BSA engine with a different timing cover and other detail changes coupled to a Burman gearbox. The frame had duplex down-tubes and a pivoted rear fork. To suit its market,

the Cyclone had high bars and chrome-plated sports mudguards.

The Leader had been announced in July 1958 and had created an immediate sensation. In a world of machines with tubular frames and construction methods rooted in Edwardian times, it struck a balance between the rider protection of the scooter and the feel and safety of the motorcycle. The design used up-to-the-minute techniques with alloy die-castings, steel pressings welded together and plastic mouldings, all held together by fastenings with Unified threads—a decade before the parent company (BSA) adopted them.

Market research had pointed to a 250 cc, twin-cylinder two-stroke, which was precisely what the Leader turned out to be, falling nicely into line with the 1961 British learner legislation. It was suggested that its designer, the brilliant Val Page, had merely copied the German Adler, which was of the same size and layout, but that machine had many different design features.

The Leader's engine was based on a single, massive die-casting which also contained the gearbox but provided an air space between the latter and the crankcase. Each crankshaft

Last of the old breed—the 646 cc Huntmaster with BSA A10 engine. For 1960, it was sold as the Cyclone in the USA

The Ariel Super Sports
Arrow, which became
known as the 'Golden
Arrow' because of its finish

Basic 1961 Ariel Arrow,
decked out for police use
with radio, but hardly a
pursuit vehicle

The Ariel Pixie shared its
engine design with the BSA
Beagle. It had more style,
but less capacity at 50 cc

assembly was separate, and both were joined in the centre with a special taper and key. Doors on each side sealed the cases, and on the outside went the alternator (on the right) together with the transmission and the points (on the left). The cast-iron cylinders were inclined forward at 45 degrees and were deeply spigoted into the crankcase. They had alloy heads with forward-leaning sparking plugs.

Due to the small size of the internal flywheels, there was another mounted just outboard of the primary-drive chain. A tensioner was fitted, as the chain ran at fixed centres to drive a multi-plate clutch of conventional British design. Where it differed was in the drum, which was formed in corrugations that provided the drive to suitably-shaped plates.

The gearbox was a normal four-speed type with the output sprocket concentric with the input mainshaft and inboard of the clutch. Its positive stop mechanism went on the right and was controlled by a pedal on the same side just below the kickstarter.

All the mechanics fitted into the one large casting, under suitable outer covers, and this was hung from the frame by one front mounting and two rear. The latter were typical lugs but the former was a single hollow lug that rose behind the cylinders with a fixing at the top. In the rear was a mounting flange for the carburettor and this led via passages to the inlet ports which were cut in the barrel spigots.

The frame was equally unique, for it was formed from pressings that made a box-section with the head races at one end and the rear suspension units at the other. This basic form was braced internally and had additional pressings welded to it to support the rear of the engine. One of these acted as the rear fork pivot, and the air filter was clipped to one side so that the frame member acted as part of the induction trunking to the carburettor. The fuel tank was simply two pressings welded together, so it was cheap and easy to make, and it was housed within the main frame box. The battery was held in a fitting bolted into the main frame aft of the tank.

To this basic chassis was added the front forks, which had trailing links concealed by pressings forming the main fork. These housed the spring-and-damper units connected to the links and the lower fork crown. There was no top crown, but the handlebars were clamped to the top of the steering column and had a pressing fitted over

them to conceal the cables. The full-width wheel hubs were of light alloy, the rear unit being driven by a chain inside a case which was not sealed but kept most dirt at bay.

This basic machine was clothed with pressed-steel panels which provided a false tank, side panels with legshields, rear enclosure and valanced front mudguard. Both wheels remained visible to reduce the effects of side winds, but the rest of the mechanics were out of sight. The false tank doubled as a luggage container, while the seat was hinged to give access to the tank filler cap, a petrol/oil mix being used for lubrication. The model had many useful features, such as front and rear brake-light switches—then very rare—locks (equally so), a lift handle and a windscreen, so it offered sophisticated motorcycling to the market. In addition, there was a long list of options, such as panniers, clock, indicators and carrier, all designed to appeal to the scooter fan and to anyone seeking to ride to work without the need for a lot of dressing up.

The Leader was a success, and for 1960 it was joined by a more conventional model called the Arrow. This had the same engine, gearbox, frame and forks, but without the panels to give the appearance of a standard machine. This worked well, despite the trailing-link forks and spine frame arrangement with its suspended engine. The false tank was revised together with the handlebars and the rear end, which gained a mudguard. In addition, the Arrow had cast-iron hubs from the start, for there had been a few problems with the alloy versions cracking. The latter were to prove marginal for solo use and not up to dealing with the extra load of a passenger.

For 1961 the engines of both models were modified with central plugs, a raised compression ratio and oval connecting rods. The cast-iron hubs became standard together with a larger fuel tank and other detail changes. A new model was the Super Sports Arrow, which had a larger carburettor, dropped handlebars, ball-end levers and a flyscreen. Its finish was largely in polychromatic gold with chrome plating and red bar grips, so it soon became known as the 'Golden Arrow'.

The range of two-strokes had detail and colour changes for 1962, and they continued unchanged for 1963. That year, they were joined by a new Ariel four-stroke, but not one that brought much joy to the enthusiasts of the older Hunter and other big machines.

The new model was called the Pixie, and its

Above **The Ariel two-stroke family, which upset the traditional owners, but was not given the necessary development for the future. Killed by BSA, the machines could have succeeded**

Left **Ariel's final indignity—the dreadful three-wheeler that did much to topple BSA**

Right **Ariel twin engine and beam frame mounting, used for all model types**

engine design was shared with the BSA Beagle, a machine intended to replace the D1 Bantam. The Pixie had a single-cylinder engine of 50 cc with overhead valves, wet-sump lubrication and a flywheel magneto. It was built in unit with a four-speed gearbox, and the primary drive was by gears, although the final drive remained a chain.

The mechanics were suspended from a spine frame built up from pressings and fitted with trailing-link front suspension. The wheels had 15 in. tyres, so their size matched the scale of the machine, which had a small dualseat, full rear chaincase and was offered with a wide range of accessories, including a screen and panniers.

Unfortunately, the announcement of the Pixie late in 1962 was not followed immediately by models in the showrooms. In fact, they did not appear until a year later. Thus, it was 1964 before many were on the road. The three existing two-strokes continued as they were, being joined by a fourth in April of that year.

The new model was the 200 Arrow, which was simply the standard machine with smaller cylinder bores and carburettor plus a colour change. This put it in a cheaper insurance class, giving potential customers an incentive to purchase it.

At the end of 1964, the standard Arrow was dropped, as most 250 buyers went for the Sports version. The latter continued together with the Leader, 200 and Pixie, but only until August 1965 when BSA decided to halt all Ariel production.

This was one of many mistakes made during that era, for in its basic form the Leader engine was right for the 1970s. Developed with more power, more gears, positive oiling and electric start, it could have been in the van of progress.

The famous Ariel name was briefly revived in 1970 for an odd three-wheeled moped. It proved a costly disaster and was one of the major causes of the collapse of the BSA group. Most Ariel enthusiasts felt it served them right!

Bond

This company was more usually associated with a small three-wheeler and, in its early days, with a small motorcycle that had a stressed-skin aluminium frame. The latter went out of production in 1953, but in 1958 the firm returned to two-wheelers with a scooter.

The first model had a 148 cc Villiers 31C engine, but it was joined by a second with a 197 cc 9E motor later in the year. They were listed as the P1 and P2 respectively. Both engines were fan cooled and fitted with a Siba Dynastart and 12-volt electrics to give push-button starting. Gearboxes were built in unit with the engine, the P1 having three speeds and the P2 four.

The engine acted as a stressed member of the frame, which had a single main tube at the front and twin tubes running up over the engine at the rear. Further tubes and pressings linked this arrangement to the back of the gearbox and provided a pivot point for the rear suspension arm, which was controlled by a single Armstrong unit on the left. Chain adjustment was by means of an eccentric pivot spindle.

Front suspension was also handled by a single arm with the spring-and-damper unit on the left, and both wheels had split rims of 10 in. diameter. They were held by six studs, and the hubs were in light alloy with 5 in. brakes. The cam spindle for each brake ran through the suspension arm, the lever and cable being outboard of it.

The bodywork was in fibreglass, the main section being equipped with a detachable panel on each side. Other parts were the separate front mudguard, weathershield, a compartment fitted to the rear of this and the footboards. Also in plastic were the rear mudguard and the fuel tank.

A hinged dualseat went on top of the main body with the tank beneath it, while the twin 6-volt batteries sat in trays on the right. The instruments were in a panel moulded as part of the weathershield and a further small moulding fitted

Above **Laurie Bond on a 1956 prototype known as the Sherpa**

Below **L. Boothman on a Bond in the 1960 Isle of Man Rally, here rounding the Gooseneck**

to the centre section of the bars. A heel-and-toe gear pedal was provided to the right, with a heel-operated rear brake pedal on the left.

For 1960 the scooters were revised and renumbered as the P3 and P4. They had the same engines, gearboxes and Siba electric starters, but these were set lower in the frame with revised mounting plates. The other major change was to the bodywork, the main section of which became a one-piece moulding, pivoted at the rear for access. This made working on the mechanics or even just checking that all was well exceptionally easy. The seat remained hinged for refuelling.

The front end was also changed with a new front mudguard that blended into and was part of the weathershield. This gave a lighter look to the machine, but otherwise they were as before.

Road tests of the P4 gave a maximum of 55 mph and easy cruising at 45, which was on a par with similar models. There were no changes for 1961 or 1962, but during the latter year the scooters were dropped from the Bond range. They were half the price of the cars the firm was making and must have been a production headache for the Preston factory, offering a much lower return. Added to that was the fact that the market was declining and their looks somehow lacked Italian flair. It was a sensible decision.

BSA

BSA must have entered the 1960s in a happy mood. They had a range which included scooters, the well-established Bantam in its original and a larger size, had a newly-introduced line of unit-construction singles, which were easing the older models out of the lists, and, to cap it all, had their line-up of popular twins.

A decade later, matters had changed considerably, but few could have foreseen what was to come. Sadly, those at the top in BSA, whose job it was to plan for the future, seemed to lack the foresight needed to make the decisions that would keep the firm going in the right direction. By the mid-1960s, panic measures began to take over from reasoned thought.

At the bottom of the 1960 range was the Dandy, which was a scooterette with a 70 cc two-stroke engine. The frame followed moped lines, having a main spine supported by short leading-link forks at the front. The fuel tank was fitted under the saddle, but it was the engine construction that was the most unusual feature of the machine. It formed part of the rear pivoted fork, the crankcase being bolted to plates which moved on the pivot, and the cylinder and head acting as the main part of the right fork leg. A bracket was bolted to the head to carry one end of the wheel spindle, and a further pressing formed the left leg.

The engine had an overhung crankshaft, and to the right of this a bulge in the case concealed the carburettor. The flywheel magneto was on the left, together with the clutch and a two-speed gearbox with preselector change. This allowed the rider to operate a handlebar gear selector, but it did not move the gear until the clutch was operated.

In use, the gearchange was noisy and often hard to put into neutral, while for novice riders the retention of a clutch for moving off proved to be one of their main problems. A combined twistgrip and clutch lever, as was common on mopeds and scooters, would have been better.

If the gearchange confused the new rider, the ignition points, hidden in the centre of the engine, were a source of annoyance to the trade. They knew only too well that the points and plug were the first things you had to check if the machine was in trouble, and many were against selling it in view of this potential problem.

Next in size in the BSA range came the 123 cc D1 Bantam, which was offered with direct or battery lighting but only with a plunger frame. The engine had larger cooling fins than the original but otherwise was the same. It was of unit construction, incorporating a three-speed gearbox, and continued to have the kickstart and gearchange pedals concentric to one another. The cast-iron cylinder was inclined forward slightly and had a simple three-port layout. The alloy head had the plug angled to the rear, and the carburettor featured a clip fitting to the inlet stub. A flywheel magneto went on the left.

The frame was a simple loop with undamped plungers at the rear and telescopics at the front. The wheels had offset 5 in. drums, and the rider travelled on a saddle or an optional dualseat. The traditional Bantam features of small toolbox, rear carrier and easily damaged centre stand (which

The BSA Dandy with inaccessible contact points and awkward gear-change—the verdict was: could do much better

was difficult to use) remained. The gear ratios and their selector mechanism were not the machine's best features, but for all that it continued to be a popular machine for getting to work.

The engine of the 172 cc D7 Bantam was very similar to that of the D1. There were internal differences, and the extra capacity was achieved by increasing the bore while keeping the 58 mm stroke that was common to all Bantam models. The obvious external change was an extra cover on the left which enclosed the generator and the clutch mechanism.

The D7 had a single loop frame with rear pivoted-fork suspension. It had heavier telescopics at the front and bigger brakes than the D1. The styling also differed, a headlamp nacelle being added to carry the light unit and provide a mounting for the speedometer and light switch. There was a much longer silencer with tapered front section, and the machine was fitted with a dualseat as standard. The area beneath the seat

Left **A 499 cc BSA Gold Star, sand racing at Wallasey in 1961; sacrilege now, but normal then**

Below left **The big BSA triple with 'ray-gun' silencer—a great motorcycle**

Below **Len Crisp and Ernie Webster, of BSA, ponder a B40 in 1961. Their wealth of experience was to be discarded in later years**

Left **BSA C15T of 1963, with revised frame and tucked-in exhaust, here fitted with lights**

Right **The first Bushman model was this D10B of 1967, which had the familiar Bantam engine**

Left **The off-road, or trail, Victor, as the B44VS of 1967**

Right **The Sports D10S was an attempt to jazz up the 20-year-old Bantam design for 1967, but it really needed something more fundamental**

nose was panelled in to conceal the battery and tools. In all, it was a machine that the Bantam enthusiast could use for long journeys as well as the shorter ones.

BSA used the D7 engine as a basis for a scooter, which was also available with a 249 cc, twin-cylinder four-stroke engine. Both versions were sold under the Sunbeam name and are described in that chapter.

Moving up the range, there were three models based on one engine—the unit-construction C15, which had been introduced late in 1958. This, in turn, was derived from the earlier Triumph Cub unit, but was enlarged to 247 cc.

As a BSA engine, it was built in conventional form with iron barrel, alloy head and overhead valves with fully-enclosed rocker gear. The pushrods ran in a separate tube, and the camshaft

was geared directly to the built-up crankshaft. Skew gears on the camshaft drove a near-vertical shaft with the points mechanism at the top and the oil pump below.

An alternator went on the left with the primary drive, which was by duplex chain to a multi-plate clutch. This drove a four-speed gearbox at the rear of the vertically-split crankcase, the output sprocket being on the left. The kickstart and gear pedals went on the right, where an outer cover gave a smooth line to the unit.

The frame had a single main loop with twin rails under the engine and pivoted-fork rear suspension. Telescopics went at the front, and both 17 in. wheels had full-width, cast-iron hubs with straight spokes. The outer rims of the hub nave plate and the brake backplate were polished to offset the overall black finish of the parts.

A headlamp nacelle carried the light unit, instruments and switches, and was a styling feature found on most of the range at that time. Mudguards were well valanced, as one would expect for a basic model, and a dualseat was standard. Beneath it, on the right, was the oil tank, which was matched by a toolbox on the left. Linking them was a centre panel, which carried the ignition switch and concealed the battery.

The road-going C15 was used as the basis for two competition models; the trials C15T and scrambles C15S. Both had the same engine with different camshaft and compression ratio, while on the outside went high-level exhaust systems—unsilenced on the scrambler.

The gearing was altered to suit the machine's purpose, as were the tyres, but the standard frame, forks and hubs were used, although the fork springs were changed and gaiters fitted to protect the seals. The fuel tank was smaller and the seat and footrests amended to suit competition use. An undershield was added. The worst feature was the energy-transfer ignition system which enabled the machines to run without a battery and have direct lighting. In use, the timing and points gap proved to be far too critical for a production competition model.

The remaining singles came from an earlier period and were pre-unit models. All were based on a common design with separate engine and four-speed gearbox set very much in the British mould.

The largest model was also the only one with side valves and a plunger frame. This was the long-lived 591 cc M21, which was built to special order and mainly bought by the AA and the armed services. It still retained its old-fashioned mag-dyno, low compression ratio and heavy flywheels to deliver a great deal of torque at a very low engine speed. It was traditional, but totally out-dated in the 1960s.

Of the overhead-valve models, the tourer was the 499 cc B33 in its final year. It had progressed to an alternator and coil ignition in place of the mag-dyno, and it came with a duplex frame featuring pivoted-fork rear and telescopic front suspension. Hubs were full width and of composite construction. The machine gave sturdy, reliable performance.

Much more exciting were the last two singles,

which were the famous Gold Stars. They were built in 348 and 499 cc capacities and were available in Clubman or Scrambler form. The former was the epitome of the café racer as it appeared in the 1950s, while the latter represented the climax of an era when scrambles machines flew high over the humps and had to be ridden by a special breed of very tough men.

By 1960 the Gold Star had reached its final form as the 348 cc DB and 499 cc DBD models. Both had all-alloy engines with large cooling fins, magneto ignition and a variety of optional pistons and cams. The gearbox was separate and offered several choices of ratio, but to the Goldie Clubman rider there was only one choice: the ultra-close-ratio RRT2 box with its needle races and the need to slip the clutch in bottom gear up to 25 mph. The scrambles box had wider ratios, and any box could be supplied with an alternative camplate to reverse the gear-change movement.

The mechanics went into a common frame which was noted for a kink in the lower right rail to clear the crankcase oil-pump housing. The remaining cycle parts were conventional with options to suit the purpose. Thus, the Scrambler had a 7 in. front brake, while the Clubman offered the choice of an 8 in. or wider 190 mm brake.

Above **A 1966 BSA Lightning twin, fresh for the road with twin instruments and sports fittings**

Above left **The army version of the B40 during a 1967 test by Peter Frazer for** *Motor Cycle*

Right **Nicely posed 1968 Lightning, with a sharp contrast in riding gear and glamour**

Left **The fast, but fragile, MkIV Spitfire of 1968—very much a model of the period**

Right **The 1969 Firebird Scrambler with exciting exhaust pipes, but little front-mudguard clearance**

The Clubman was set off by its clip-on bars, lovely swept-back exhaust pipe, special tapered silencer that gave a characteristic twitter noise on the overrun, and plenty of chrome. The only colour came from the maroon lining on the silver panels and the large, round Gold Star badges on the tank. Both speedometer and rev-counter were fitted by nearly all owners, and behind them was the steering damper knob. This was locked in position by a spring clip held by the standard handlebar clamps. The layout of this area at the top of the forks characterized the model.

The Scrambler did not follow quite the same line as the Clubman, for it had a normal exhaust pipe and a smaller fuel tank. Normally, its oil tank was fitted on the right side under the seat nose, but a central tank was available as an option. This model's future was less secure, as the world was moving on to lighter and more compact scramblers, usually with two-stroke engines or smaller four-strokes, such as BSA's own C15S. Neither looked as imposing as the Gold Star.

The rest of the BSA range were twins, and for road use there were tourers and sports models in 497 and 646 cc capacities. The former were listed as the A7 and A10 Golden Flash, and the latter as the Shooting Star and Super Rocket. All had a great deal in common, having the same cycle parts and gearbox, and engines which were based on the same design.

The engine was a classic vertical twin, with the gear-driven camshaft set to the rear of the crankshaft so all four pushrods moved in a tunnel at the back of the iron block. Alloy heads were fitted to the sports models, but the tourers had iron versions, although all were constructed in the same way. All models had a single carburettor, a magneto which was gear-driven from the camshaft and installed behind the block, a dynamo strapped to the front of the crankcase where it was chain driven, and the same timing side and oil pump.

The gearbox was of the type fitted to the pre-unit singles, and the frames were similar but without the kink in the lower right rail. The telescopic forks had the headlamp nacelle common to other models, and full-width, composite hubs were used. A single bolt held the petrol tank in place, a dualseat was standard and a full rear chaincase was available as an option.

The final twin was the export A10 Spitfire, which followed the lines of the earlier Rocket Scrambler. This machine had the Super Rocket engine with open exhausts run at waist level on the left. The cycle side was off-road with tyres, seat and mudguards to suit; no lighting equipment was fitted. In effect, it was the twin-cylinder equivalent of the scrambles Gold Star, but it must have taken plenty of muscle to keep under control.

All except the B33 went forward into 1961

without any notable changes and were joined by two new models. The first of these was the 343 cc B40, which was very similar to the C15 but had a pushrod tunnel cast in the head and barrel, a valve lifter, 18 in. wheels and a 7 in. front brake. Most of the details were the same as on the smaller model, the extra capacity rounding out the performance.

The second new model appeared in April 1961 and was geared to suit the new laws restricting learners to 250 cc. It was a sports machine listed as the SS80 Sports Star. Although it offered an increase in engine power and some other internal changes, it was otherwise much as the C15. The result gave a performance similar to that of the B40, but from a high engine speed and with a more noticeable cam effect. Just what a learner could do without.

There was more news for 1962 when three new twins appeared, while the singles and existing twins continued. All the new models were important, and one was destined to become a favourite classic. This was a super sports edition of the A10, known as the Rocket Gold Star.

The idea for this machine had come from well-known Gold Star specialist Eddie Dow, who had been asked by a customer to fit a Rocket engine into a Gold Star frame. The result was a very nice sporting motorcycle, so the idea and a list of standard parts used to do the job was taken to BSA late in 1959.

All was quiet for two years until Dow had a call from BSA to say that they had lost his list and to ask for another as they were going to take up the idea. The result was the RGS, but in the process the idea of using stock parts had also been lost, the frame and mudguards, together with other parts, being special to the one model.

Despite this, it was a handsome machine and was normally kitted out with clip-ons, rearsets and both speedometer and rev-counter, just like the single. The parts used for this were also listed as options for the Super Rocket, and this model is often mistaken for the genuine RGS, as they can look alike. The frame number will reveal which is the real one.

If the RGS was for the café racer, the other two new twins were for the tourer and were, in fact, the first of a range of unit-construction models which were to replace the existing twin line-up. Announced in January 1962, the two machines were the 499 cc A50 and 654 cc A65.

Both models were lighter than the old machines and both had many common parts, with just a change of bore size to give the two capacities. The engine was smooth and clean, but really it was the old design in new clothes, for the layout of the crankshaft, camshaft, timing gear and oil pump were as before. New were the alternator on the left and the coil-ignition points set in the right-hand outer cover.

Internally, there were improvements, and both models had alloy heads. A triplex primary chain was used to drive the four-speed gearbox which was contained within the crankcase castings, but this also owed much to the past.

The cycle side was nearly identical on both machines, the frame having duplex down-tubes and a pivoted rear fork. The telescopic front forks had the BSA nacelle for the light unit, speedometer, ammeter and twin switches, while full-width hubs were fitted with 7 in. brakes, except for the A65 which had an 8 in. front stopper.

The mudguards were well valanced, and some degree of enclosure was provided by very large side covers which hid the carburettor as well as concealing the oil tank, toolbox and battery. The single bolt fixing for the petrol tank continued, and the large chainguard could be replaced with an optional full chaincase.

The new twins were quite well received but, although they offered good motorcycling with only a few detail faults, they did not represent a real move forward as one would have expected from a new design. This was not surprising, as they were really developments of the old models with some weight removed. In time, they were to experience some rather major internal problems.

The final new model for 1962 did not appear until May and was the sports version of the B40. It was listed as the SS90 and followed the same lines as the smaller model with tuned engine and revised gear ratios.

At the same time, the two C15 competition models were modified with an alloy tank and mudguards, 7 in. offset front brake and improvements to the ignition system. The scrambler was given strutted bars and an expansion-chamber tail to the exhaust pipe.

The Dandy was dropped at the end of the year together with the two versions of the A7 and the 348 cc Gold Star. A new model was announced for the bottom end of the range. This was the 75 cc Beagle, which had the same engine as the Ariel Pixie described previously, but bored out to increase the capacity.

While the engine and gearbox units of the Beagle and Pixie were virtually the same, in other aspects the machines differed considerably. The Beagle had much more of a moped style, its spine frame being built up from pressings with the fuel tank perched on top. The rear pivoted fork was a part of the styling, not half concealed as on the Ariel, and the front forks were of the short leading-link type. Its overall appearance was rather old-fashioned and suggested the mid-1950s rather than the early 1960s.

Although the Beagle was announced late in 1962, its production was delayed, and it was late 1963 before it reached the showrooms. There, it had to compete with a foreign newcomer—the Honda 50 scooterette, which offered both performance and weather protection.

The rest of the BSA range continued as before, the only real changes being to the C15 competition models which were given new frames. These had a central oil tank and duplex seat tubes that allowed the exhaust system to tuck inside the right-hand one. At the end of 1963, there were more changes, and a number of older models finally disappeared from the lists.

First was the D1 Bantam, which had served so many for so long. Next was the big Gold Star and the side-valve M21. It was also the end for the A10 and its derivatives, including the Rocket Gold Star, despite the niche it had carved with the café racer fraternity in two short years. Somehow, the unit twins were never to gain the affection riders had shown for the older model, or that machine's stylish and purposeful lines.

By now, all of the range were of unit construction and included some new models for 1964. At the bottom was the Beagle, followed by the D7, still in battery or direct-lighting form. Then there were the unit singles with 247 and 343 cc models in touring and sports form, plus the two 247 cc competition versions. There were also off-road machines in both sizes for export, and these were based on a combination of the road engines and competition frame. Most went to the USA, but they also sold well in Australia and in other countries where riding on trails was as common as being on tarmac.

The two basic twins continued and were joined by others for both home and export markets. For the former, there was the A65R, which was a sports version of the 654 cc twin. This had an increased power output, better clutch and siamezed exhaust system, while the appearance was enhanced with chrome-plated blade mudguards, similarly finished headlamp supports and fork gaiters.

For the USA, the A65R became the A65T/R Thunderbolt Rocket with high bars and small tank, while for even more performance there was the twin-carburettor A65L/R or Lightning Rocket. The side panels on the latter were abbreviated to make room for the two instruments feeding the engine.

In addition to these road models, the US market was also offered the A50 Cyclone Competition and A65 Spitfire Hornet, which were off-road machines in the two capacities with twin carburettors, open exhausts and no lights.

There was one new single for 1965. It was listed as the B44GP and known as the Victor Grand Prix. It was based on the works scrambler ridden to two world titles by Jeff Smith and was an out-and-out competition machine with an all-alloy engine featuring a hard chromed bore and linked to a tougher gearbox. This was fitted in a frame where the tubes acted as the oil tank. The forks were new and were to appear on all the twins in 1966.

There was one major change to all the unit singles for 1965, and that was the repositioning of the points in the timing cover. At the same time, the clutch mechanism was changed to a rack-and-pinion. There were other internal detail alterations too. The only single that differed from this was the Bantam, which soldiered on with little change, as did the Beagle.

The 1969 441 cc Shooting Star road-model, which was easier to ride than the smaller Starfire, but forbidden to learners

The twin range became a little confused, although the three basic domestic models continued much as before. They were joined by sports versions with splayed inlet ports carrying twin carburettors and listed as the Cyclone A50C and Lightning A65L. These basic sports machines had Clubman variants, listed as the A50CC and A65LC, and these were fitted with a close-ratio gearbox, rearsets, racing seat and dropped bars.

The off-road models continued, so there was still an A50 Cyclone competition (or A50CC—hence the confusion) and the Spitfire Hornet. Missing from the line-up was the A65T/R, as the US buyers preferred the twin-carburettor A65L/R which was continued as a result.

There were major changes to the range for 1966, and at the bottom of the scale the Beagle was dropped. The Bantam models were joined by a pair of low-cost versions given the name Silver.

The C15 competition models, B40 and SS90 were dropped, but the C15 road version carried on, and the SS80 became the C15 Sportsman with humped seat and separate headlamp shell. The B44GP was retained and was joined by the off-road B44VE Victor Enduro, which had the C15 competition frame and a detuned 441 cc engine with linered barrel.

The twin range was simplified and reduced to six models, two of 499 cc and four of 654 cc. The basic

Above **The BSA Starfire of 1970. Its performance was rather too much for the novice rider**

Right **A Rocket 3 on show in 1970, with a Dalesman to the rear, hence the Puch symbol**

road versions were still much as they were in 1962 but were listed as the A50 Royal Star and A65T Thunderbolt. For off-road use, they became the A50W Wasp and A65H Hornet but, again, were little changed from previous years. The last two models were sports machines, and the first was the A65L Lightning, which was continued from 1965 but with twin exhausts in place of the siamezed variety. The second was the Spitfire Mark Two Special and was in the style of the A65LC, but its Hornet engine was fitted with Amal Grand Prix carburettors in place of the Monoblocs used on off-road versions.

During 1966, the D7 Bantam was replaced by the D10, which was built in four forms and continued for 1967. All had a new, improved alternator on the left, while the points were moved to the right beneath a small cover in the primary chaincase. Internally, there were changes to increase the power and an extra clutch plate to cope with it.

The basic models kept the traditional three-speed gearbox and were listed as the Supreme and the low-cost Silver. New to the range was the Sports, which had the long-awaited four-speed box and a fresh appearance. This came from a humped seat, flyscreen, waist-level exhaust, full-width hubs and special handlebars. The final Bantam model was the off-road Bushman, which had trail tyres, revised gearing and an undershield.

The other change during 1966 affected the internals of the C15 models, which gained the more robust Victor bottom half. This was of limited use to the Sportsman, which was dropped at the end of the season. In its place came the C25 Barracuda, which presented a new image and some unusual design features. Chief of these was a one-piece crankshaft with plain big end, while the appearance was changed considerably thanks to a square-finned barrel, sculptured petrol tank and shapely side covers. The engine specification was high performance with hot cams and a high compression ratio, while the sporty looks were helped by a humped dualseat.

The C15 continued alongside the C25 for 1967, as did the Victor Grand Prix and Enduro models. They were joined by the B44VS Victor Special and B44VR Victor Roadster, while the C25 was also built as the B25 Starfire for the USA. The Roadster was very much like the Barracuda, but its 441 cc engine gave it the same performance with less effort. The special was for off-road or street-scrambler use and was very similar to the Enduro which it was to replace.

The six twins continued for 1967 with a finned rocker-box cover and other detail changes. As a result, the Spitfire became the MkIII, and then the MkIV for 1968. At the same time, the off-road 650 changed its name to the Firebird Scrambler A65FS, the Wasp was dropped and the Royal Star, Thunderbolt and Lightning were re-equipped with Concentric carburettors. The one other noticeable alteration for 1968 was to the front brake on the Lightning, Spitfire and Firebird, all of which were fitted with the twin-leading-shoe type.

The two-stroke became the D14 for 1968 and

was built in three forms, all with the four-speed gearbox. These were the Supreme, Sports and Bushman. They were the same as the D10 models they replaced except for a fatter exhaust pipe. The Barracuda was only listed as the B25 Starfire, while the 441 cc road model became the B44SS Shooting Star and the B44VS was continued. Both Grand Prix and Enduro models were dropped, as was the C15.

If the singles range was smaller, there was a new multi at the top end to become the flag bearer. This was the 740 cc Rocket 3, which mirrored the Triumph Trident, except that its cylinders were inclined forward a little and the timing-side covers were shaped to give a flowing line. The engine design had come from the Triumph works at Meriden and, in essence, it was a Triumph twin with another cylinder added on.

The engine's crankcase was similar to the pre-unit Triumph twin, with a massive centre casting added between the two halves. This incorporated the two centre mains, making four in all, and extended back to enclose the gearbox. The camshafts went fore and aft of the block, being gear driven in Meriden style, and the pushrods passed through tubes, as on the twin.

Both head and block were one-piece components cast in alloy, and most of the construction was straightforward, although the alternator was located on the timing side and the oil pump driven from the left end of the crankshaft. The points were at the end of the exhaust camshaft, which also drove the rev-counter through a set of gears. A trio of Concentric carburettors fed the mixture into the engine, and the exhaust system was a three-into-four-into-two arrangement. This came about because the centre pipe split and ran into the two outer ones, which then swept round to individual silencers. Each of these terminated in a plate with three outlets, and they were soon labelled 'ray-gun' silencers. The gearbox had four speeds and was driven by a triplex primary chain and diaphragm clutch.

The engine and gearbox unit was mounted in a frame with duplex down-tubes and which differed from that used by the Trident. The rest of the machine was 'state of the art', as seen by the group at that time, and used common forks and hubs together with a twin-leading-shoe front brake. The side covers were special to the model, as was the petrol tank, which had an oil cooler under its nose.

For 1968 the A75, as it was listed, was offered for export only, and it was 1969 before the home

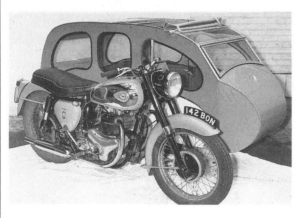

Above **A pair of Beagles on a leash, showing their 1950s moped lines, in marked contrast to the Ariel Pixie**

Left **Very traditional A10 with enormous Canterbury Carmobile three-seater sidecar in 1961—made obsolete by the Mini two years earlier**

market could try it and discover what a good machine it was. On the major aspects of speed, acceleration, handling and braking, it earned high marks, but it was let down by minor niggles. By the time it reached the home market, the cable and lever of the front brake had been amended, as they had been on all the twins equipped with that particular brake type.

Otherwise, the twins were continued, minus the Spitfire, which had effectively been replaced by the Rocket 3, so there were only four models. They had a new alternator and had gained an oil-pressure switch, while the 654 cc Thunderbolt,

Lightning and Firebird had been given an exhaust balance pipe.

The singles continued, with the twin-leading-shoe front brake appearing on the road-going four-strokes. A more prosaic version of the B25 was also added to the range. This was the Fleetstar, which had a more subdued performance and plainer finish for fleet users such as the police or post office. The Bantam range was reduced to two models in standard and Bushman form, but with revisions to the engine. At last, this had a central sparking plug together with many internal changes that would take the engine to its final form.

The entire range, less the Fleetstar, continued for 1970 and was subjected to a final major revision for 1971, which played a great part in the company's downfall. However, the 1960s closed with BSA's two-stroke, three unit singles, four twins and the triple in forms that buyers preferred.

Butler

Chris Butler owned a company which made a wide range of fibreglass parts for manufacturers and riders, and in 1963 he decided to build a complete machine. His prototype was a trials model with a frame built from square-section tubing, as were the leading-link forks—other than the rear loop, which was of round section. Pivoted-fork rear suspension was employed, and both ends were controlled by Girling units. The engine was a 246 cc Villiers with a Parkinson conversion to the top half. It was linked to a four-speed gearbox.

Naturally, the fuel tank, front mudguard, one-piece seat pan, rear mudguard and air-filter box were in fibreglass. The hubs were Motoloy, and the rear brake was cable operated. The machine was intended to be light and came out at 210 lb.

A year went by, and in 1964 a trio of scrambles models were to be seen with round-tube frames but with the same forks as on the trials prototype. Engines varied; the Spartan was fitted with the 246 cc Villiers 36A, while the Spitfire had the same unit with a Parkinson top-half conversion. Finally, the Star-rider had the 247 cc Villiers Starmaker engine with a single carburettor, rather than the twin units fitted as standard.

A few weeks later, two trials models were announced, both to be sold in kit form. These had common cycle parts and had returned to square-section tube for the frame, retaining the leading-link forks. They were very similar to the prototype, except that a small fuel tank was fitted.

The engines were from Villiers, the Tempest having a 246 cc 32A with iron barrel, wide-ratio gearbox and heavy flywheel. The Fury differed in having a Parkinson top half conversion on the same engine. Options for the machines included a larger fuel tank, prop-stand, rock guard, snap-action filler cap and red or blue finish for the fibreglass parts.

Butler machines were built in limited numbers, but they sold well until the industry as a whole declined further, and eventually they ceased production.

247 cc Star-rider machine and Butler mouldings on show at Earls Court late in 1964

Cheetah

Machines that carried the Cheetah name were built by Bob Gollner in small numbers for trials use. As production began in the 1960s, it was inevitable that some would be powered by A-series Villiers engines and that a number would have square-barrel conversions fitted.

The square barrel was one option, but others included the Villiers Starmaker engine in its trials form, the Triumph Tiger Cub and the Swedish Husqvarna. Later on, when the supply of Villiers engines dried up, Gollner went on to use Japanese units to keep the machines in production.

All engines were fitted to a conventional set of cycle parts: tubular frame, slimline telescopic front forks, pivoted-fork rear suspension and trials equipment. Various brake forms were used, including a front disc, and the general standard of construction was very high, as is usually the case in small production set-ups. They were very functional machines indeed.

The simple, functional Cheetah frame, which took a variety of engine units

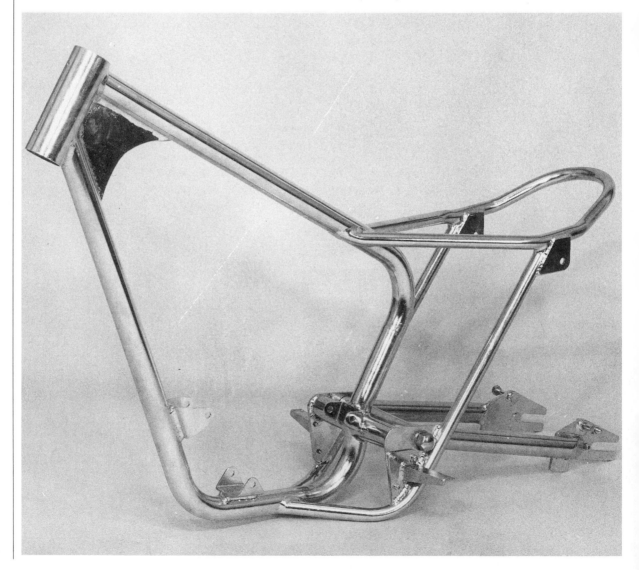

Cotton

Cotton entered the 1960s with a small range of five models: three for the road and two for competition. In addition, there were two more road models available to special order, and these alone did not use Villiers engines.

The basic road model was the 197 cc Vulcan fitted with a Villiers 9E engine and three-speed gearbox. This had a loop frame with pivoted-fork rear suspension, while at the front there were short leading-link forks. Both front and rear suspensions were controlled by Armstrong units, and a deeply-valanced front mudguard was fitted.

At the rear, the area between the dualseat nose and the rear number plate was fully enclosed by sheet-steel pressings that extended downwards to near the wheel spindle. These were joined at the front, being secured to the rear mudguard and the pillion rest supports. A small lifting handle was provided behind the dualseat. Both full-width hubs had 6 in. brakes.

The other road models were very similar, both having twin-cylinder engines with four-speed gearboxes. The smaller model was the 249 cc Herald with a Villiers 2T engine, while the larger 324 cc Messenger had a 3T unit. The latter differed in having 7 in. brakes and a 21 in. front wheel, which was an unusual feature on a road model.

Both special-order machines had Anzani twin-cylinder, two-stroke engines and were the 242 cc and 322 cc Cotanza models. The engines had an unusual plain centre main bearing, which also acted as a timed inlet port. Both were dropped during the year.

The range was completed by two competition machines, which used the road frame braced with extra tubes and without the rear enclosure. The forks had an extra brace in the form of a tubular loop to join the two leading links. These models were the 197 cc Trials, with 9E engine, and the 246 cc Scrambler, with 33A engine. Both had a four-speed gearbox and 6 in. brakes.

The range was expanded during 1960, the first addition being the 249 cc Double Gloucester,

Cotton Scrambler, which was new for 1960, with a 246 cc Villiers 33A engine and Armstrong forks

Left **Cotton Vulcan for 1960, with 9E engine, leading-link forks and some crude rear enclosure**

Left **The 1962 Messenger twin with 324 cc 3T engine and neater panelling**

Below **Cotton Cotanza with the Anzani twin engine that had a centre main inlet port**

which appeared in April. It was based on the Herald, but in a more sporting vein, with the competition front fork, narrow chrome-plated mudguards, low bars, small screen and much reduced rear enclosure. The engine was the same 2T unit, although high-compression heads were promised. The riding position proved more tiring over any distance.

Then came a Vulcan Sports in the same style, but with the 9E engine and the choice of a three- or four-speed gearbox. This option also became available on the standard Vulcan. For this model, either the full or shortened rear enclosure could be specified.

This made up most of the range which went forward for 1961 unchanged, but there was more to come. A further competition model was produced by simply fitting the 246 cc 32A engine in place of the 9E to make the Trials 250. At the same time, the Scrambler was given the option of a 34A engine in place of the usual 33A.

Next to appear was the 249 cc Continental, which followed the lines of the Double Gloucester but had a new duplex frame, the tuned engine, a small headlamp shroud-cum-flyscreen and Italian wheels with light-alloy hubs. These were full width with 180 mm front and 160 mm rear brakes.

The final new model did not appear until April and was the 246 cc Corsair, which had the Villiers 31A engine. This was fitted in the single-loop frame with Continental wheels, shroud and partial rear enclosure, but it had the normal handlebars.

The entire range continued for 1962, the Scrambler being listed with the 34A engine only and no other changes. This made a total of ten models, and they were joined by one more called the Cougar. This was a scrambler too, but with a duplex frame, new hubs with 6 in. brakes and a special engine.

The Cougar's engine was based on a Villiers 34A, but it had a Cross barrel and piston. These were very different from normal conversions of this type, as the barrel was aluminium and neither sleeved nor hard chromed in the bore. The piston was supported in the bore by a special composite piston ring and two steel bands which were rivetted to the skirt. The ring was in two parts, each with seven turns that were wound on to the piston. One part acted as a ring land and the other presented a knife-edge to the bore. The cylinder-head and exhaust-port seals were also unique Cross designs, for that company specialized in sealing rings.

In June, an experimental Cougar was seen fitted with a Villiers Starmaker engine, and later a Cotton with a modified 34A appeared in a road race. These two events cast their shadows over the 1963 range, for when it was announced it included two new models.

Both machines were powered by the 247 cc Villiers Starmaker engine, which was a major step forward for that firm. It was much more up to date than the other engines, but in both Cotton models it had a curious twin-carburettor arrangement. These fed the single inlet port, but the slides opened in turn for a good pick-up. This engine came with a four-speed gearbox only.

The scrambles Cotton was called the Cobra, while the road racer was named Telstar. Both shared a new duplex frame fitted with the scrambles leading-link forks and full-width hubs. Fixtures and fittings were to suit each bike's purpose, so the former had knobbly tyres and the latter a dolphin racing fairing, although it too had a 21 in. front wheel.

The rest of the Cotton range was much as before, but the Vulcan was listed with the three-speed gearbox only, while the Sports version retained the option of a four-speed. The other road single was the Corsair, and beside it ran the Herald, Double Gloucester and Continental twins. The last was joined by a Sports version with detail alterations. The larger Messenger twin continued, but with a duplex frame and 19 in. wheels.

On the competition front, the Trials and Trials 250 ran on, being joined by the Trials 250 Special, which had a Parkinson conversion on its 32A bottom half and some chassis alterations. The Cougar continued in the Cobra frame, but with a Parkinson conversion on its 36A instead of the Cross parts, while the basic Scrambler was dropped.

The range was reduced at the end of the year, the Vulcan, 197 cc Trials, Double Gloucester and Continental all being dropped. This left the Vulcan Sports as the sole 197 cc machine together with the Continental Sports, the Herald, the Corsair and Messenger to continue for 1964, but the last three were to special order only for 1965. The Trials 250, Trials 250 Special, Cougar, Cobra and Telstar also continued, the trials models being given a duplex frame.

In June 1964, the Telstar became the Mk2, and when the 1965 models were announced there were further changes. One was that the two 249 cc twins were fitted with the 4T engine in

Top **The road-racing Cotton Telstar in 1964 at a damp meeting**

Above **1965 Cotton Cougar scrambler with Parkinson square-barrel conversion on its 36A engine**

place of the earlier type. Additions to the range were the Starmaker Trials and Conquest, both with the 247 cc Villiers engine.

The engine in the trials model was adapted to its job and fitted in a duplex frame similar to that of the existing trials machines. The Conquest was for road use and built in sports fashion, as were the Vulcan and Continental. The two trials models and the Cougar continued, as did the Cobra, but this last was dropped during the year.

One further item in the firm's list was a frame kit, which was based on the 500 cc Triumph-engined machine being successfully scrambled by Arthur Lampkin. Cotton offered the frame, leaving the customer to provide the engine, wheels and front fork. Norton telescopics were the first choice, as the headstock was designed to accept them. The idea of supplying kits had come up in 1963 when the scrambles models were offered in this manner, and by 1965 it had extended to the trials machines as well.

For 1966 the road range was reduced to the Vulcan Sports, Continental Sports and Conquest, and there were five competition models. These comprised the two trials machines with 32A and Starmaker engines, the two scramblers and the Telstar road racer. One scrambles model was the Cougar, still with its 36A engine featuring a Parkinson top half, but to special order only. The other was the Cobra Special, which retained the Starmaker engine, but had new forks and a lighter frame.

The three road models were continued for 1967, and the Telstar gained a new frame and lost some weight, partly through a switch to 18 in. wheels. The frame was a duplicate of that used by works rider Derek Minter, who had had a great deal of success with his machine in British races.

The competition models were offered with the option of Metal Profiles telescopic front forks in place of the usual leading-links, and the machines

A road Cotton with the Starmaker engine—the 1965 Conquest with sporting mien

Cotton Continental with the Villiers 4T twin engine for 1965

were only sold in kit form. Only one scrambler remained as the Cobra Special, but there were two trials models with a new, lighter frame and leading-link forks. One was the Trials Starmaker, but the other was listed as the Trials 37A, being a replacement for the old Trials 250. Its Villiers 37A engine could be supplied in standard form or bored out to 262 cc with piston and ports to match.

At this time, the company fell victim to two setbacks that were beyond its control. The first was a change in the law, preventing customers from escaping purchase tax by buying a machine in kit form. This removed much of the advantage that kit bikes had enjoyed. The second was the demise of the Villiers engines. The 37A unit was built for a while, but the range came to an effective end by the middle of 1968. During that last period, the Cobra was renamed the Cossack.

These events halted production until 1973, when the name was revived for a range of competition models fitted with Minarelli engines. Later still, it was used for a road racer with a Rotax engine, but in time this was taken over by Armstrong.

The Cyclemate, which had the Cyclemaster powered wheel in Norman cycle parts, but it was outmoded by the 1960s

Cyclemaster

The Cyclemaster company was perhaps best known for its powered bicycle wheel, which was a direct substitute for any cycle's existing rear wheel. This arrangement differed from the other cycle attachments of the day which, in the main, operated through a friction drive to a tyre.

The device was crammed into a drum which formed the hub of the wheel. It comprised the engine, two-stage transmission with clutch, and fuel tank. The exhaust system ran round the flywheel magneto housing, being tucked in well.

Originally, the engine was of 25.7 cc, but later this was bored out to 32.6 cc. In both cases, a disc valve controlled the inlet. For 1955 the same engine was fitted to a complete machine called the Cyclemate.

Cycle parts were made by Norman, the open-pattern frame having twin top tubes that ran through to the rear spindle. The engine was mounted in front of the bottom bracket and drove the rear wheel by chain. Brakes were under 4 in. and there was no suspension. With only cycle tyres and the saddle for comfort, the machine's low performance was easier to accept.

The Cyclemate just made it into 1960, but by then its job was being done more efficiently by the many mopeds that were available, so it was discontinued from the middle of the year.

Dalesman

Dayton

Dalesman was formed in 1968 to build off-road competition machines, using the Austrian Puch 125 cc engine. The machines, for trials, scrambles and enduros, had many common parts, both from the Puch road model and purpose made.

A duplex frame carried the well-finned engine with its unit-construction four-speed gearbox, and both forks and wheels were Puch. The seat, tank and silencer were special, while the detail fittings were to suit the model's sphere of activity.

Early on, it was found that the Puch forks were not up to the strains of competition, so these were changed to REH units. This improved that area, and the machines continued to be built up to 1974. However, the trials model was never as good at its job as the other two.

Another firm that only just made it into the 1960s was Dayton, most of their machines having been produced during the last half of the 1950s. For 1960 there were just three models, all scooters and all called Albatross. Two shared the same bodywork and were of 250 cc, but one was a single and the other a twin. The third model had a smaller, single-cylinder engine.

The smaller machine was the Flamenco, which had a 174 cc Villiers 2L fan-cooled engine with three-speed gearbox and electric starting. The frame and bodywork followed typical scooter lines and were produced in conjunction with Panther and Sun, so all three makes had a similar appearance, but this arrangement did spread the tooling costs. Most differences were in the front end and detail finish.

Access to the mechanics was provided by a large, detachable panel on each side, and the top of the engine could be reached by lifting the side-hinged dualseat. All the normal service items were within easy reach too. This aspect was improved further by the easy manner in which the rear body section could be removed, giving complete access to the engine for repair or removal.

At the front end, the apron carried a fascia panel for the speedometer, ammeter and light switch. In the rear of the apron there were two storage compartments, the right-hand one being lockable. The front suspension was by leading links, the spring units being mounted outside the fairly large mudguard, which moved with the wheel. At the rear, there was a pivoted fork.

Gerald Rathmell on the Dalesman, with its 125 cc Puch engine, riding in the 1969 Scott trial

The other two models had old-fashioned styling and a heavier, taller appearance. There was a pronounced tunnel between the apron and the rear body, while the lower part of the engine was visible on each side.

The power unit of the Continental was the 249 cc Villiers 2T twin-cylinder engine with four-speed gearbox, while the Continental Single had the 246 cc Villiers 2H engine. The latter was a single with four-speed gearbox, being replaced by the A-series engine after a short life, but not in the Dayton.

The chassis was tubular and the suspension was the same as on the Flamenco, as were the fascia panel and the two storage compartments in the back of the apron. The bodywork was heavier but, again, the rear section had side panels and was easy to remove completely, while the seat was also hinged.

Machines in the Dayton range, especially the Continental models, were faster, heavier and perhaps steered better than the Italian scooters, but somehow they lacked the flair of their rivals. They offered features and a performance that were probably in excess of those demanded by the average scooter rider, and this limited sales. Sadly, the entire range was discontinued late in 1960.

Diamond

The Diamond name dated from before World War I, but the late-1960s machines that used it had no other connection. They were off-road competition models aimed mainly at the American trials market, for which they were more to a trail format.

There were also trials and scrambles machines in small numbers for the home market. These, and the American machines, were based on a duplex frame housing a 125 cc Sachs engine with five speeds. REH telescopic front and pivoted rear forks provided the suspension, while the rest of the equipment was to suit each model's use.

The machines were well thought out and executed, but seem to have been built in limited numbers.

Dayton Albatross in its original 1956 form with a 225 cc engine, replaced by a 250 cc single or twin for 1960

DKR

The DKR company only built scooters with Villiers engines, and for 1960 they offered four models, all with the same basic frame and bodywork. The frame was based on a single, large-diameter tubular backbone, which ran from the lengthy headstock to a point beneath the engine. A subframe was welded on to carry the rear suspension and support the engine cover and seat.

Both front and rear suspensions were based on pivoted forks, the former arranged in leading-link form. They were controlled by twin spring units and hydraulic dampers. Pressed-steel wheels of 10 in. diameter were used. The fuel tank was located in front of the headstock to improve weight distribution, and the controls were conventional, with a rocking pedal for the gearbox.

The bodywork was massive at the front, there being a pressing which blended with the apron to run forward and support the light unit, enclose the fuel tank and shroud the front wheel. The rear of the machine was also enclosed with detachable side panels, and a hinged dualseat gave access to the mechanics. A large glove box was attached to the back of the apron.

There were two 148 cc models, both of which had Villiers 31C engines with fan cooling and three-speed gearboxes. The main differences were that the Dove MkII had direct lighting and a kickstart, while the Pegasus had a Siba Dynastart and a starter button. In addition, the Dove frame was modified to place the starter pedal in a lower position, this facility not being needed on the other model.

A larger model was the Defiant, which was fitted with a 197 cc Villiers 9E engine with fan cooling, electric starting and four-speed. Like the Pegasus it closely resembled, it had twin batteries in a tray beneath the dualseat. The final model was the Manx which had a 249 cc twin-cylinder Villiers 2T

engine, again fan cooled with electric starting and four speeds. As this engine was wider than the single, the side panels were dished for clearance and had more louvres to provide extra cooling. Its batteries were fitted one on each side under the panels.

During the year, there was a change to the Pegasus, which became the MkII in May, following installation of the 174 cc Villiers 2L. In other respects, it stayed the same, but it was only built up to October, when it was dropped from the range together with the Dove MkII. Their place was taken by a trio of new models all bearing the name Capella and listed as the MkI, Standard and De Luxe.

The MkI Capella had the 148 cc 31C engine with three-speed gearbox, but the others used the 174 cc 2L with four speeds. All had fan cooling, and the De Luxe also had electric starting, 12-volt electrics and warning lights for ignition, neutral gear selection and low fuel.

The Capella models had a new frame and bodywork, which dispensed with the distinctive but heavy nose of the older machine. In its new form, the front pressing ran just above the wheel and could be fitted with a small carrier, which was offered as an option. The rear side panels were larger, and styling overall was sharper.

Although the frame was new, it was similar to the earlier type, with a massive backbone, long headstock and welded-on subframe. The front suspension was the same as before, but at the rear there was a pivoted arm on the left with a stub axle for the rear wheel and a single spring and damper unit. Wheels were as before, but the fuel tank was under the dualseat.

The 197 cc Defiant and 249 cc twin Manx were continued in the old style, but only until September when they were also dropped. In their place came one further model in the new style, which retained the 197 cc 9E engine from the Defiant. This was the 200 Capella De Luxe. In other respects, it was the same as the 174 cc De Luxe model.

This range of four scooters was unchanged for 1962, but in July 1963 it was joined by a 200 Capella Standard, which was simply the 174 cc model fitted with the 9E engine, a kickstart and 6-volt electrics. In these forms, the five models continued until production ceased early in 1966.

Top right **The DKR frame with forward fuel tank, which dictated the heavy body line**

Above **Bob Currie road testing a 1963 DKR Capella 200KS, which had a lighter style**

Above **Earlier DKR body style, which was distinctive, if nothing else**

DMW

By 1960 the DMW firm, based at Sedgley in Worcestershire, had an unusual range comprising one scooter, a road single, two road twins and both single- and twin-cylinder competition models. All were powered by Villiers engines and all, except the scooter, had a four-speed gearbox.

The scooter was called the Bambi, and it had a 98 cc 6F engine with fan cooling and a two-speed gearbox. This assembly was bolted into a tubular subframe which, in turn, was fitted into the pressed-steel body. The latter was in scooter style with hinged single seat and a tunnel between the apron and the rear body.

Front suspension was by a long leading fork, its supports being concealed by a massive front mudguard. The fork spring was inside the steering column and was attached to the fork itself by a stirrup. At the rear was a pressed-steel pivoted fork. Both wheels were of disc form and 15 in. diameter with drum brakes.

The road single was the Mk9, which had a 197 cc 9E engine installed in a DMW P-type frame. This was constructed from square-section tubing, a feature of the firm's frames from 1951, with a pressed-steel centre section which extended back to support the rear suspension units, dualseat and rear mudguard. Compartments within the pressing accommodated the battery and tools, access being gained by raising the dualseat.

Front suspension was by telescopic forks with the option of a pivoted-fork system. The latter was used at the rear. Less usual for a small model was that chain adjustment was achieved by moving the entire fork to and fro. A full chaincase was fitted.

The brakes, which were new, were installed in full-width hubs. They were based on a Girling design which activated the shoes through an S-cam and two tappets. Adjustment was carried out at the pivoted end of the shoe, using a wedge expander and two further tappets. The rear wheel was quickly detachable.

The twin-cylinder models were the 249 cc Dolomite II and the 324 cc Dolomite IIA with 2T and 3T engines respectively, both with the option of Siba electric starting. The cycle side was the same as the Mk9.

DMW Deemster with extended screen and canopy for police use in 1965

In addition to the road models, there was a variety of competition models, all based on one frame and forks. Engine choices in the Mk12 were the 246 cc 32A for trials and 33A for scrambles, with the option of the 9E suitably tuned and geared for the machine's purpose. The Mk10 had the 249 cc 2T engine, again tuned to suit. The frame, built from square-section tube, had pivoted-fork suspension at front and rear.

Except for the 9E option on the Mk12 competition models, the entire range continued unchanged for 1961, which was hardly surprising, as the firm had a new model to launch in January. This was the Deemster, which combined the merits of both motorcycle and scooter in an unusual manner. The overall layout, riding position and handling were taken from the motorcycle, but added to them were the enclosure, weather protection and small wheels of the scooter.

Two models were listed as Standard and De Luxe, and while both had a 249 cc 2T engine, the latter had electric starting. The engine was fitted in

Above **DMW Bambi scooter with 98 cc Villiers 6F engine and dreadful rear brake pedal**

Below **The 1963 DMW Mk16 scrambler with Starmaker engine**

the normal motorcycle position to ensure correct weight distribution and was not enclosed. The frame comprised large-diameter top and seat tubes, bolted-on square-section down-tube, a large box-like structure and a peripheral framework.

The box structure was bolted to the seat tube and ran back to support the tops of the rear suspension units and the dualseat. Inside, there was enough room for two 1960s-style helmets, and there was a separate space for the toolkit. A rear mudguard extension was bolted to the back of the structure.

The peripheral framework supported floor panels in scooter style and was bolted to the down-tube, the seat tube and to stays attached to the rear mounting points. It was extended to run round the tail of the machine and act as a support for the end of the rear mudguard.

Rear suspension was by pivoted fork and, in typical DMW style, this had snail-cam adjusters at the front end for tensioning the chain. The actual pivot point was in the seat tube. Front suspension was similar to the Bambi, with a pivoted fork and stirrup link to the spring inside the steering column. The spring medium was rubber in compression, and movement was damped by a

hydraulic unit attached to the right-hand fork leg. The fork support was concealed by an impressive front mudguard.

Interchangeable 12 in. diameter wheels were fitted. They were of the pierced-disc type and cast in light alloy. The wheels were mounted on hubs with 6 in. Girling brakes of the type used by the motorcycles. The chain driving the rear wheel was fully enclosed.

The bodywork was in scooter style, with detachable side panels that enclosed the area from the rear of the engine to the tail of the machine. There were footboards along each side and a pair of substantial legshields, which had small stowage areas at their tops. The legshields blended into the sides of a motorcycle-style tank that sat above the engine in its usual place.

Ahead of the tank was a further cowl which carried not one, but two headlamps. The cowl was on a pivot, and an adjuster allowed the headlamp beam to be set easily. Either one or both lamps could be turned on, and the dip switch controlled both.

The machine was unique and defied attempts to categorize it.

Not wishing to rest on their laurels, the firm turned its attention to the competition models.

Left **DMW Deemster fitted with police radio, pictured at Dudley Priory in 1962 with Mike Riley, Harold Nock and Bob Currie**

Right **A DMW with Starmaker engine for road use. It was built for trade assessment late in 1965, but never reached production**

The Mk10 and Mk12 machines were dropped, and for 1962 there was a Mk14 scrambler, with 34A engine, and a Mk15 trials, with a 32A. Both were of 246 cc and had four-speed gearboxes.

The frame for these two machines was completely new and had moved away from the square-tube concept. It was based on a large top tube and tapered down-tube, both welded to a headstock containing taper-roller head races. A subframe and fabricated seat pillar frame were bolted to the main portion, and a pair of plates ran under the engine to complete the structure.

Suspension was pivoted fork front and rear, but chain adjustment was achieved by moving the wheel rather than the fork. Both hubs had 6 in. Girling brakes, but at the rear the scrambler had a cush-drive and right-hand brake, while the trials model had a rigid hub and left-hand brake. This caused the rear suspension units to be fixed above the wheel spindle on the trials machine and ahead of it on the scrambler.

Detail equipment varied with the machine's purpose, but on the trials engine the exhaust pipe was run in an inverted loop ahead of the cylinder before running to the silencer. This was to achieve the required pipe length. The scrambler had a stub exhaust, massive air cleaner and racing plates.

In addition to its standard 34A engine, the scrambler was also offered with a light-alloy barrel incorporating a liner with matt chromium on the bore. This came with an alloy head, Hepolite piston and four waisted studs to secure the parts.

Of the other models, the Bambi was dropped, but the two Deemsters were continued, as were the 197 cc Mk9 and the two Dolomite twins. The road motorcycles retained their telescopic front forks and the optional pivoted-fork arrangement.

During 1962, the trials and scrambles models were offered in kit form to save the customer from paying purchase tax. The scrambler could be had without the engine, in which case the engine plates could be left blank or cut to order. Later in the year, the 324 cc Dolomite IIA was dropped, and the 249 cc II was joined by a Sports Twin with tuned engine, lowered bars and light-alloy mudguards.

Late in the year, DMW took over Ambassador, and the two ranges were rationalized to some extent. This did not happen at once, so the K-series of Dolomite standard and Sports twins continued, and they were joined by the rather similar M-series models. The same thing occurred with the Mk9 and M series Mk9 machines with the 9E engine, but the two Deemsters ran on, together with a

Above left **The Mk2 DMW Hornet for 1966 with Enfield top half**

Left **The 1965 DMW Dolomite II with Villiers 4T engine**

police version. The last had a radio and blue lamp among its extra equipment. As a result of the machine's low centre of gravity, it was easy to ride at near zero speed.

On the competition front, there was more activity, the Mk14 and Mk15 being replaced. The scrambler became the Mk16 and had the 247 cc Starmaker engine, while the trials model was the Mk17 and retained its faithful 32A. The alloy-barrel conversion remained in the lists as an extra for this engine.

A new competition machine was the Hornet road racer, which also had the Starmaker engine, as did others of that period. This followed standard practice as regards the frame and suspension, and it came with a fairing and screen. Within weeks, it had been well track tested and revised accord-

ingly. The original built-up frame was altered to an all-welded assembly, and dual front brakes were fitted. The telescopic front forks retained a single suspension unit mounted above the wheel, but they had detail changes. The exhaust was unusual, comprising an expansion box under the engine joined to a short, round silencer with twin tailpipes, one on each side of the rear wheel.

The range was altered further for 1964, the K-framed Mk9, Dolomite and Sports Twin being dropped. This left the same three models in M-frame form, but for the twins there was an engine change to the Villiers 4T unit. The same change occurred on the Deemster models, which were listed as the Kickstart and Electric Start versions.

For competition use, the Mk17 trials model was continued and was joined by two scramblers, one being the Mk14, which reappeared with a 36A engine. Both machines continued to be listed with the alloy-cylinder option. The Starmaker scrambler became the Mk18 with a new, all-welded frame, and the Hornet continued with a single GP carburettor and expansion-box exhaust system.

DMW changed their minds on frame construction once more for 1965, returning to the K-type and square-section tube for the Dolomite. The Sports Twin remained with the M-frame, but the standard twin in this frame was dropped, as was the 197 cc model. The Deemsters continued, as did the Mk17, Mk18 and Hornet for trials, scrambles and road races. The Mk14 scrambler was replaced by the Mk19, which had the 36A engine in a duplex frame and was also available with the alloy engine conversion.

Late in 1965 came news of a road racer with a twin-cylinder engine based on two Starmaker units coupled together. One or two prototypes were built, and later still one was assembled with Enfield top halves on an Alpha crankcase. None of these ever reached production.

The range shrank rapidly at the end of the year, as the firm turned to more general engineering work. They continued to make the Metal Profiles forks, which had been one of their products when the DMW marque had first appeared in 1950, and they were still making these in the 1980s.

The 1966 range comprised the Dolomite Sports Twin, the Deemster Kickstart and the Hornet racer. The last came in two forms: one much as before, but with a five-speed gearbox, the other with an Enfield top half and the five gears. The Deemster was also built with the Velocette Viceroy 247 cc, flat-twin, two-stroke engine.

By August, production of the road machines had ceased, and only the Hornets continued for 1967. During that year, they were dropped too, and the firm effectively ceased motorcycle manufacture. They did continue to produce spares and the occasional trials model with their own development of the 250 cc single-cylinder engine. The spares, together with Villiers parts and the forks, continued to be offered, the operation being revived in the 1980s.

DMW Highland Trials model of 1967, with Cotton frame and 37A engine

Dot

The 'Devoid of Trouble' company began to build motorcycles in 1903, and they won a TT in 1908. They continued with two wheelers until 1932, but then turned to three wheels, first with pedal power and later with Villiers engines. In 1949 the firm returned to motorcycles, applying most of their effort to competition machines. These appeared as works models in the 1951 125 cc TT. At about the same time, Bill Barugh became the works rider in scrambles.

The small 197 cc Dot scrambler soon began to harass the bigger machines, and before long Bill was ahead of the large-capacity works teams from BSA and AMC. Customers were not slow to realize that the light, cheap two-stroke was a much better bet for the average club rider, as it had enough power to make him think yet did not have all that tiring weight. Dots began to sell very well, and this success was augmented by recruiting Eric Adcock to ride a trials model with similar effective results.

By 1960, however, the firm's best days were over, Greeves becoming more dominant. Even so, Dot offered a seemingly extensive range that year. In truth, many models were essentially the same with either engine changes or the addition of road equipment. Thus, the six 197 cc machines were duplicated by six more with 246 cc engines.

All but one model that year were competition orientated, which allowed the firm to concentrate on essentials and ring many changes through the provision of a range of options. They also acted as agents for the Italian Guazzoni road models, which gave them a couple of machines to display, and they were involved with 48 cc Dot-Vivi machines in moped, scooterette and racing form.

The genuine Dot models all had their Villiers engine with four-speed gearbox in a loop frame with pivoted-fork rear suspension controlled by twin suspension units. Their short leading-link forks were also controlled by twin suspension units, and all models had 6 in. brakes front and rear. All but the road model had a 21 in. front wheel, and most had a 19 in. rear, although some had 18 in. rear wheels. Fittings were provided to suit the specific competition use. Among these were massive mudguard clearance, small fuel tank (with an alloy option for some), short seat and tucked in, high-level exhaust system.

The Dot 350 SCH Twin, which had the RCA engine, designed by Peter Hogan, with its side-mounted exhaust stubs

The 1960 Dot 246 cc Trials Works Replica, with Villiers 32A engine, was very functional

The scrambles models were built in three forms for each capacity, the 200 SCH and 250 SCH being stripped ready for racing. Engines were the 197 cc 9E and 246 cc 33A, with close-ratio gearboxes fitted as standard, although others were always an option. The other scrambles models were the SH, which had road equipment, a silencer and speedometer, and the SDH, which was the same but had direct lighting.

This sequence was repeated for the trials models, which had the 9E and 31A engines, but with wide ratios in the gearbox. The basic model was the THX, while the TDHX had direct lighting.

The supply of lights, even on the scrambler, was a practice continued from the immediate postwar years. In those days, it was normal to ride a trials machine, and often a scrambler, to the event, remove the lights and any other unwanted gear, compete, refit everything and ride home. In time, the use of trailers and vans for transporting competition machines became far more usual, and equipment reflected that trend.

There were two further trials models in the Dot list: the 200 and 250 Trials Works Replica. The larger model was fitted with a 32A engine. On both machines the footrests were further back, and there were other detail alterations to make them pure trials bikes with little regard for any need to run them on the road.

The final two models in the range were rather different, as they were both powered by the 349 cc twin-cylinder RCA engine. This had been designed by Peter Hogan who, with brother John, had been very successful on Bantams in British 125 cc racing during the early 1950s. The engine concept was modern, with a horizontally-split crankcase and full flywheels, but the cylinder block was in iron with the exhausts at its outer edges. A four-speed gearbox was bolted to the back of the engine, and some units had Siba electric starting.

Dot used the engine to power the Sportsman Twin, which was built as a road model with coil ignition and full equipment. A tuned engine went into the 350 SCH Twin, still with coil ignition, to

Left **The 1962 Trials model, back with square-section main frame tube**

Left **The 1961 Trials Works Replica, with round-tube frame replacing the earlier square-section version**

Right **Dot trials model for 1963, with a few more changes**

produce a scrambler, but the power curve, which was fine on the road, was of little use on the rough. There was nothing low down to haul a rider out of trouble.

Much of the extensive Dot range was dropped at the end of the year, allowing the firm to concentrate on a few basic machines. Out went all the 197 cc models and the two twins, as did all the 246 cc machines, except the SCH and the Trials Works Replica or WR. These continued with just two other models, the 200 and 250 Trials Marshall. Engines for the last two were the 9E or 32A, and the machines were very similar to the WR, but they were fitted with direct lighting, a dualseat, pillion rests and a smaller-section rear tyre of 19 in. diameter in place of the 4.00 × 18 in. version on the WR. The 250 SCH changed to a 34A engine, and all models had a chain oiler incorporated in the rear fork leg, alloy mudguard stays and chainguard, and a slimmer, lighter fuel tank.

There was one further model, called the Californian, which was intended for export. It was built in enduro form with a large tank holding over 4 gallons, a scrambles engine, fat front tyre and lighting equipment.

Most of this range was dropped at the beginning of 1962, including the 200 Trials Marshall which brought the line of 197 cc Dots to an end. The 250 cc version also disappeared, but the WR carried on. In March the 250 SCH was replaced by a new model called the Demon Scrambler. This had a Villiers 34A engine with a light-alloy barrel conversion as standard, although the stock parts could be retained as an option. A

close-ratio, four-speed gearbox was specified, and there was a wide selection of overall ratios to suit different courses and conditions

The Demon Scrambler's frame was new and was constructed from square-section tubing in the usual loop form with a welded-on subframe. The pivoted rear fork had legs of the same section, but the front forks were the usual leading links. Both wheels had full-width hubs with 6 in. brakes, the front wheel having a 21 in. diameter, while the rear was 18 in. The fuel tank was in light alloy, as were the mudguards and oval competition plates. A large, twin-element air cleaner was fixed to the Amal carburettor.

During 1962 a trials prototype with the square-section frame was run in the Scottish Six Days, and at the end of the year the Demon International appeared. This exercise resulted in a modified WR for 1963 which had the new frame and a number of other changes to reduce weight. Among these were lighter Armstrong units to control the front forks, although the rear end continued under Girling management.

A Demon Scrambler was modified with the 247 cc Villiers Starmaker engine with four-speed gearbox and twin carburettors feeding its single cylinder. The square-section scrambler frame was used together with the same forks, wheels and other details. However, it failed to reach production, so the model with the 246 cc engine ran on, but with a 36A engine. In May 1963 this two-model range was joined by the Special Alloy Works Replica trials model, which was simply the WR with an alloy barrel conversion and Amal carburettor.

The three models were continued for 1964, and were available in kit form as well to avoid purchase tax. For 1965 they were joined by the Special Demon scrambler, which had the alloy cylinder on an Alpha bottom half, effectively creating a new engine. The crankshaft had full flywheels and was a good deal stiffer than the old Villiers unit, so it was much more efficient at coping with the power from the barrel. The gearbox remained unchanged, but ignition was by a Miller or Stefa magneto with external coil. Again, the machine was available assembled or in kit form.

At the end of 1965 the Demon Scrambler was dropped, but the other three remained for 1966. The Special Demon became the Demon Scrambler Mk3 early in 1966, being provided with a revised cylinder, piston, exhaust system, footrests and frame. In July it was joined by the Mk4, which had a gearbox with cam-barrel change and a duplex primary drive to relieve two previously overstressed components.

Both the Mk3 and Mk4 were replaced by the Mk5 at the end of the year. This had more power due to an improved exhaust system and changes to the porting. The WR was renamed the 250 Standard Trials and its engine was changed to the 37A, while the Special model continued as it was.

There was one new model for 1967 in the form of the 360 Demon Scrambler Mk5, which was the same as the 250 but with a larger engine. It had appeared in mid-1965 as a 250 with oversquare dimensions. The bottom half had four bearings to support the full-circle flywheels in an Electron crankcase. The magneto was on the right under a cover, and a light-alloy cylinder with cast-in liner was fitted. Porting was conventional for the time, with one inlet, one exhaust and two transfers. A four-speed gearbox with cam-barrel change was bolted to the engine, and the complete transmission was heavy duty to cope with the loads. The engine was bored out to 360 cc and installed in the current scrambles frame.

All four models continued for 1968, but from April they were only supplied in kit form. Relations with Villiers had become rather strained as the firm replaced more and more standard engine parts with Alpha units or their own items. In the end, the supply of engines dried up as Villiers became enmeshed in the NVT turmoil, and Dot could only keep going by turning to foreign engines and other work. The final models had Minarelli engines, and they continued with these until 1977. However, by then, the firm was more involved with Armstrong suspension units.

Dot Works Replica trials model for 1966, with alloy-barrel conversion and Amal carburettor

Dunstall

Paul Dunstall arrived on the motorcycling scene at the beginning of the café racer era and soon carved a niche for himself as the man for Norton twins. Although later he was involved with many other makes, he made his name with the Bracebridge Street models, and this activity stood out in a sea of Triumphs.

Dunstall raced a carefully prepared Norton 99 in the late 1950s and was an immediate success with it. However, he did not continue to race for long, as his main interest was in preparation. Consequently, at an early age, he became a sponsor while working in the family motorcycle business.

To suit the requirements of his race engine and improve the machine's ground clearance, he had fitted swept-back exhaust pipes, and before long these were in demand by the owners of road machines. This opened up a market that he found he had to himself, as no-one else was racing a Norton twin with much success. Soon the pipes were followed by engine tuning parts, and later by just about all the special cycle items demanded by the café racer.

By 1961 Dunstall offered a catalogue full of special parts, and as well as selling a host of Norton items, he began to branch out into other makes, providing a range of silencers for all manner of machines. He seized any opportunity to expand the business and kept his name to the forefront by supplying 650 racing twins to some of the front runners on the British short circuits. They responded with enough wins to gain plenty of publicity.

In 1964 he began to sell fully-modified Norton twins under his own name, and they came with most of the special parts already fitted at a price that was little more than that of the standard model. They sold well, for they gave the customer exactly what he wanted in an era of road machines that followed the racer image. Within a couple of years, Paul was viewed as a small manufacturer, and in 1967 the ACU accepted that fact. Thus,

The Dunstall Metisse with 745 cc Norton Atlas engine, Oldani front hub, and Manx forks and rear hub, as built for successful road racing

Dunstall racing models and some of Paul's special parts, on show following his 1968 successes

Dunstall became a proprietary make, allowing Paul to enter machines in the big production races where they were very successful.

Dunstall continued with the Norton frame until the power he was obtaining became too much for it, so he tried his engine in a Rickman Metisse frame. Later, he fitted a 500 cc engine in a Lyster frame as a further experiment. For 1969 he moved on to a new spine frame to cope with the power from the tuned 745 cc engine, but by then he was more involved in engine tuning kits for the Commando. He had produced these for the launch, and as the decade came to an end was moving more and more in this direction together with the production of accessories for machines of British, European and Japanese origin.

His work was characterized by its sound engineering and first-class finish, regardless of the make or model he was dealing with. Dunstall Dominators were no longer built in 1970, but the Commando parts continued and were joined by many others for most of the major marques sold in the 1970s.

Elstar

The Elstar name came from a combination of Alf Ellis, the founder, and BSA Star, as his early grass-track machines were built to take that unit. The name was best known for kit machines for speedway or grass-track use and designed for the BSA or a large JAP single-cylinder engine running on dope. The latter had a very long history and was basic, simple, sturdy and easy to maintain. It had magneto ignition, total-loss lubrication and overhead valves with an all-iron top half, which the methanol fuel helped to keep cool.

For speedway, there was a countershaft, but the grass-track kit had a gearbox. The frames were open loop, and the front forks telescopic with rubber-band suspension. Fittings were minimal and comprised the essentials only.

In the mid-1960s the firm also offered trials machines in kit form to take a variety of engines. Their construction was mainly conventional with a single-tube open frame, telescopic forks and pivoted rear fork, but there was a bolted-on cradle under the engine and gearbox. This allowed unit BSA single, Tiger Cub, Villiers, Bantam or other similar engines to be used, simply by selecting the appropriate cradle. In addition, the headstock accommodated taper-roller races and would take BSA, Triumph, Metal Profiles or Ceriani forks, while the rear fork allowed some variation in the hub employed. For the rest, the fuel tank was small and slim, the seat short and the mudguards minimal.

The machines were all successful in their chosen sphere, but sadly Alf Ellis was killed in a car crash and the firm died with him.

An Elstar grass-track machine fitted with a unit BSA engine—simple and potent

Excelsior

The Excelsior company differed from most of those making lightweights in Britain during the post-war years by not relying totally on Villiers engines. Instead, they made some of their own. By 1960 some of these had been dropped, but half of their range of eight models still relied on the home-grown product.

At the bottom end of the range were the F10 and C10 Consort models, both of which had the 98 cc Villiers 6F engine with its two-speed foot-change gearbox. The F10 was a true utility model, for the engine unit was carried by a simple, rigid, tubular frame, which had slim girder forks when announced in April 1959. These looked like telescopics, as the main members were tapered tubes, but suspension was by links with a single, central spring. For 1960 they were changed to light telescopics with gaiters.

The machine was completed with low cost in mind, being supplied with direct lighting and a saddle but without a speedometer, which was not a legal requirement. However, one was available as an option.

The C10 was very different, despite having the same engine, as it had pivoted-fork rear suspension, valanced mudguards and full-width hubs. In addition, there was a degree of enclosure for the centre section of the machine, and a dualseat was provided.

The next machine in the range was the U10 Universal, which was a conventional model fitted with a 148 cc Villiers 31C engine and three-speed gearbox. Ample side covers enclosed the central area of the frame, and both mudguards were well valanced. The R10 Roadmaster was very similar, but was fitted with the 197 cc Villiers 9E engine, although it retained the three gears. It also had the same full-width hubs with 5 in. brakes, but had a slightly larger fuel tank.

The two remaining motorcycles were both twins with Excelsior engines. Smaller of the two was the 243 cc TT6 Talisman Twin, while the larger machine was the 328 cc S9 Special Talisman. Both engines had a common stroke and a three-part crankcase with vertical joints. These were on the cylinder centre-line, so the centre casting formed the inner half of both cases, the two outers acting as covers.

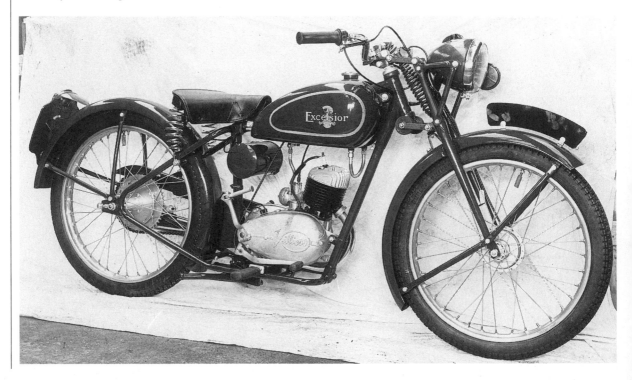

Six bearings supported the two crankshafts, which were keyed together in the centre and assembled to the centre casting. The outer web on one side was added before the cover was fitted. The rest of the design was conventional, with separate iron cylinders and alloy heads. A four-speed Albion gearbox was bolted to the back of the engine.

The Talisman dated from 1950, the original model having been improved over the years. With the passage of a decade, the TT6 had acquired pivoted-fork rear suspension and a dualseat, so it was similar to the R10. The larger S9 twin differed in having twin carburettors, extensive rear enclosure panels that hid the top half of the wheel, and a cowl at the top of the front forks. Both twins had 6 in. rear brakes, but the S9 had a 7 in. front unit, while that of the TT6 matched its rear.

The final two models were the Monarch scooters, both of which had 147 cc Excelsior engines with three-speed gearboxes. The MK1 was the cheaper, as it had 6-volt electrics and had to be kicked into life, but the ME1 had 12 volts and a Siba Dynastart to go on the button. In fact, both machines were DKRs, having the same frame but with bodywork that had been altered to take the Excelsior engine and name badge.

This arrangement allowed the firm to test the market, but the experiment ceased in the middle of the year. The undisguised DKRs were dropped, being replaced by totally new Excelsior designs which did, however, retain the original engine.

The two machines still carried the Monarch name and were listed as the K11 and E11 with kick and electric starting respectively. Both continued with fan cooling and three-speed gearboxes. At the front end, the frame was similar to that of the DKR Capella, as were the leading-link front forks and rear pivoted arm. This had the same method of chain adjustment as the DKR, together with the stub axle for the rear wheel, but the rear subframe differed.

The fibreglass bodywork was all new, the rear section being easy to lift clear of the machine to give access to the mechanics. The seat was hinged so that the filler cap and sparking plug could be reached. Footboards ran forward to the apron, which carried the headlamp, horn and a fascia panel, and had the fixed front mudguard bonded to it. The result was not only smarter but also 50 lb lighter than the earlier model.

The scooters continued unchanged for 1961, as did most of the motorcycles, although they were recoded. Thus, the Consorts became the F11 and C11, the Universal the U11, the Roadmaster the R11 and the Talisman twins the TT7 and S10. There were three new economy versions listed as the EC11, ER11 and ETT7, the last of these having simpler battery and toolbox panels. Also new was the E9 Golden V scooter, which was based on the

Left **Excelsior 98 cc Consort model with 6F Villiers engine in F-series utility form, without rear suspension or much at the front**

Right **Excelsior Monarch scooter, which used the DKR frame and body but had the 147 cc Excelsior engine**

Above **The Super Talisman Twin with the larger 328 cc Excelsior engine**

Below **The Excelsior Universal 150, shown on the half-title page, assembled and ready to roll in 1962**

The 1963 Universal model, which had a 31C Villiers engine in place of the earlier Excelsior unit

Monarch but fitted with a 197 cc Villiers 9E engine with fan cooling, four speeds and electric starting.

During 1961 the market was seen to decline, and the Excelsior range began to contract. In May the TT7 was dropped, followed two months later by the C11 and R11. September saw the last of the U11, E9 scooter, ER11 and S10.

This left a smaller range for 1962, but the two Monarch scooters continued as the K12 and E12. The economy 243 cc twin became the ETT8, and it was joined by the 328 cc ETT9, so the larger twin also lost its rear enclosure. At the bottom of the range, the basic Consort became the F12, while the other became the EC12.

Early in the new year, a seventh machine appeared. This was the U12 Universal with the 147 cc Excelsior engine. It was unusual in that it was supplied in kit form and thus was exempt from purchase tax. This saved the customer nearly £36 and left him with the relatively simple task of putting the sub-assemblies together, which was no more than a leisurely morning's work.

The resulting machine was a neat, no frills, sturdy model suitable for local use. The concept was successful, and the option of a 148 cc Villiers 31C engine was also offered. For 1963 this became the standard fitting; and the machine was redesignated the U14. This self-assembly scheme was also extended to include the de luxe Consort, which became the C14. Originally, the machines would have been numbered U13 and C13, but the error of such a label was soon realized and the sequence of numbers was moved on one.

The rest of the range was dropped, which meant an end to the twins and scooters as well as the basic Consort model. The two remaining machines continued for 1964, but the days of motorcycle production were drawing to an end, and the long-running Consort was dropped late that year. The Universal followed during 1965, bringing the marque to an end. However, it was to reappear briefly in the late 1970s on a mini-bike.

Firefly

The Firefly frame kit was designed in the late 1960s by Phil Jones and Brian Newberry to take Villiers engines or, with minor changes, the Husqvarna or Greeves Challenger units. The machine was conventional in form and well made, having a number of features that ensured easy access and maintenance. Details were simple and well thought out.

Parts for the Firefly came from various sources and included Bultaco front forks, Armstrong suspension units and British Hub wheels. The rear chain was adjusted by eccentrics at the wheel spindle, and the ignition coil was protected from vibration by simply wrapping it in sponge and pushing this package into a hole in the air box. The easily-adjusted footrests had two height positions, and the fuel tank was small to keep the centre of gravity low and prevent it getting in the rider's way.

This was a nice machine which showed the designer's skill and enterprise, but like many others of that period, the company was only operating on a small scale. It was dependent on the advantage of selling machines in kit form to avoid purchase tax, and when this disappeared (followed by the arrival of VAT), the business died.

The Firefly frame kit—simple, well made and well thought out

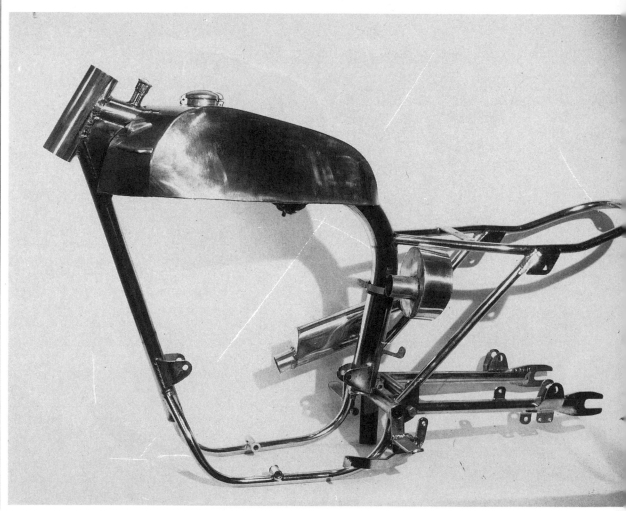

Francis-Barnett

As part of the AMC group, Francis-Barnett turned their backs on Villiers engines at the beginning of the 1960s in favour of the group's own two-stroke engines, which were fitted to their entire range. At first, the move was restricted to a simple engine replacement, but in time new models appeared from the outset with AMC power units. Eventually, however, the company returned to using Villiers engines for twins and competition machines.

For 1960 the range comprised seven models beginning with the 149 cc model 86 Plover. Its engine was of conventional design but was arranged so that the cylinder could be vertical, inclined or horizontal to suit the particular engine installation. This was achieved by rotating the entire crankcase relative to the gearbox shell. The latter contained three speeds.

The power unit was fitted in a simple loop frame with a pressed-steel rear enclosure, which concealed the forward-mounted rear springs. This made for a clean, functional style that hid such items as the battery. There were telescopic forks at the front. Full-width hubs, with 4 in. front and 5 in. rear brakes, were used, and the machine was finished with a good-sized petroil tank and a dualseat.

Francis-Barnett publicity photo of the model 79 Light Cruiser with 171 cc AMC engine

Above **This Falcon 87, of 1960, continued the lengthy use of the model name, but introduced the 199 cc AMC power unit, which was not good news**

Above right **The well-enclosed Cruiser 84, on show at Earls Court with the largest of the AMC engines**

Right **Francis-Barnett model 82 Scrambler with superb Norton forks and unreliable 249 cc AMC engine**

'249 c.c. Cruiser 84   £199.12.8d.
(inc. £34.2.8d. P.Tax)
Chrome Tank £4.2.7 extra

150cc SPORTS FULMER 90
£149-0-0
(INC. P. TAX)

Above **The strangely styled Sports Fulmar 90 showing its unusual frame construction, 149 cc AMC engine and leading-link forks**

Above right **Francis-Barnett 92 Trials model of 1963, with Villiers 32A engine—a great improvement, until supplies dried up**

Right **Last of the Plovers was this 1964 model 95, which kept to the 149 cc AMC engine, surmounted by a humped tank**

Next in size was the 171 cc model 79 Light Cruiser, which also had a degree of rear enclosure but in a different style. The engine unit was of a streamlined form with vertical cylinder and alloy head. Its construction followed normal practice in most respects, although the head fins were set in a radial pattern. Another unusual feature were the transfer ports, which lacked the normal inner wall, being simple grooves in the bore. The piston had ports in its sides and a crown that was shaped to guide the gases, matching deflectors cast into the cylinder head.

A Lucas alternator supplied the current and an Amal carburettor the mixture. The gearbox was bolted to the rear of the crankcase, but the two were blended into one unit by the shape of the casting and the outer side covers. Primary chain drive was used, and the box had four speeds with foot-change.

This power unit was fitted in a composite frame assembled from pressed-steel down- and seat-members plus tubular loops. Pivoted-fork rear and

telescopic front suspension was provided together with full-width hubs containing 5 in. brakes front and rear. A smart tank and dualseat set the model off, and the sides were enclosed by panels that ran from the rear of the cylinder back to the subframe tube. Well-valanced mudguards also played their part in keeping the rider clean.

The 199 cc model 87 Falcon had the same engine as the 171 but with an enlarged bore. The suspension and hubs were the same too, but the frame was a tubular loop type and the electrics

were Wico-Pacy. There was less enclosure with more conventional side panels to conceal the battery and tools, and the machine followed the concept of the many earlier Falcon models as a simple 200 cc motorcycle.

The four remaining machines had engines based on the 249 cc AMC unit with four-speed gearbox. They comprised the Cruiser models 80 and 84, the Scrambler 82 and the Trials 85. The engines of the last two were modified to suit their purpose, as were the gearbox ratios. The 82 had a Wico-Pacy energy-transfer ignition system, while the 85 had a quickly-detachable lighting set.

The basic engine design was similar to the 171 and 199 cc units (in fact, it preceded them), so it was well streamlined and conventional, apart from the transfer ports and deflectors. It also had the radial head fins. The carburettor was enclosed by a small cover with a rubber boot to seal the cables.

The basic Cruiser 80 was similar to the Light Cruiser 79, having a composite frame, but in this case with an oval-section down-tube, pressed-steel mid-section and tubular rear loops. The suspension was also similar, as were the full-width hubs, but they had 6 in. brakes.

The 84 was based on the 80, but with the addition of extensive weather protection. This took the form of a well-valanced front mudguard, legshields and complete enclosure of the machine aft of the cylinder. Even the pillion rests folded in to present a flush exterior.

The two competition models had tubular loop frames and Norton front forks. Both brakes of the Trials model were 5 in., but the Scrambler had a 6 in. front. This machine also had a short, open exhaust, but the trials version ran at waist level on the right-hand side to a silencer tucked out of harm's way behind the frame tube and rear suspension unit.

There were no changes for 1961, other than the removal of the model 79 from the list to leave six machines which were continued for 1962. For that year the Cruiser 84 lost its legshields, while the 80 was offered with the option of a rear chaincase. In addition, there were two new models, the first of these being the model 89 Cruiser Twin, which marked a return to the use of a Villiers engine. This was the 249 cc 2T twin-cylinder unit with four-speed gearbox. It was slotted into the Cruiser 80 cycle parts with virtually no changes.

The second new model was very different in style and was listed as the 149 cc model 88 Fulmar. It had the same engine as the Plover, but by then it

was being assembled by Villiers at their Wolverhampton works.

The frame, forks and styling of the Fulmar were all different to the normal Francis-Barnett approach. The first was essentially of the spine type, featuring one main tube which ran from the headstock, over the engine and round the back of the gearbox, to a point beneath the power unit. Light tubes formed triangles to carry the seat and rear suspension unit supports in a bolted assembly that was reminiscent of the company's pre-war methods.

At the front were short leading-link forks with a massive crown beneath the headstock to support the pressed-steel blades. Both wheels had full-width hubs with 5 in. brakes and well-valanced mudguards. On top of the frame was a body assembled from pressings. It supported the headlamp at the front and ran from there to the tail of the seat. The fuel tank was a simple box beneath the seat, which was hinged at the rear to allow refuelling and provide access to the battery, while the dummy tank had an access panel for a stowage box. The battery was a simple dry-cell version on the direct-lighting model, but a wet battery and rectified charging were available at extra cost.

The Plover was dropped at the end of the year, together with the two competition models and the enclosed Cruiser 84. The Fulmar, Falcon, Cruiser and Cruiser Twin continued for 1963 with detail changes, and they were joined by four new models which were seen first at the Earls Court show.

Smallest of the new models was the Sports Fulmar 90, which was similar to the 88 but with four speeds, flyscreen, polished alloy mudguards and a bright finish. Many of its features appeared on the Sports Cruiser Twin 91, which was further enhanced by an Italian 'jelly-mould' style tank and rearsets with a remote gear linkage.

The other two models were replacement competition machines with Villiers 246 cc engines instead of the AMC units. Both had four speeds, but with wide ratios for the Trials 92, which had a 32A engine, and close ratios for the Scrambles 93, which had a 36A engine with a Parkinson square-barrel conversion. Otherwise, the two models were the same as before.

Further changes occurred for 1964, and the Cruiser 80 was dropped. The Fulmar, its sports version, the Falcon, and the two competition models continued unchanged, but the Cruiser

The final
Francis-Barnett was
the 1966 model 96,
which was simple,
basic transport, even
lacking the familiar
bird name used by
the firm for so long

Twins were fitted with the Villiers 4T engine in place of the 2T.

There was a revised Plover model 95, which retained the 149 cc AMC engine and three speeds, but in a single-tube spine frame with telescopic forks, full-width hubs with 5 in. brakes, and a stumpy fuel tank. During the year, the Scrambler 93 had its engine replaced by the 247 cc Villiers Starmaker unit, becoming the model 94.

No changes were announced for 1965, and by then most models had a counterpart in the James range, for in 1962 Francis-Barnett production had been moved to the Greet factory. Thus, the machines were built side by side and inevitably grew closer and closer in all except superficial external details.

At the end of the year, the two Fulmar models were dropped, while the Plover, which had been revised to become the model 96 earlier in 1965, continued for 1966. In its new form, the engine unit was fitted in a simple, conventional loop frame. The Falcon and Cruiser Twin were exclusive to the Francis-Barnett range and ran on, while the Sports Twin and two competition models all had James equivalents.

None was altered, as by then the firm's days were numbered due to the troubles of the parent group, and in October 1966 production ceased. This was a sad day for many riders who regarded the firm as one which built a rather better machine than some of its contemporaries.

Gaunt

When Suzuki linked up with Alta to build a mini trials machine, they decided not to supply Peter Gaunt with engines for his projected replicas. His reaction was to cut free from them and switch to a tiny 89 cc Jawa two-stroke engine to power his machine.

The Jawa came in unit with a five-speed gearbox and was hung from a spine frame with down-tubes for protection only. Everything about the machine was small and light, the weight being under 150 lb, which made it easy to handle. Less helpful was the engine, which was a disc-valve type offering high performance but little bottom-end power. This made it difficult to ride successfully for the average clubman, but with Gaunt aboard it won the Irish Experts trial.

The Gaunt was cheap, so quite a few were sold in 1969 and 1970, before other makes began to take its place in the market.

Peter Gaunt and his 89 cc Jawa-powered mini trials machine, which had a spine frame

Greeves

By 1960 Greeves were very well established as builders of competition and road machines. In that year Dave Bickers won the 250 cc European Moto-cross title on a Greeves, and was to go on to take it for a second time in 1961.

The Greeves range for 1960 reflected the firm's interests and, in the main, was devoted to competition models, all with their characteristic cast-alloy frame beam and leading-link forks. Construction of the frame began with the top tube being welded to the headstock, which had three weld beads laid round it to prevent it bowing. This assembly was placed in a sand mould and the molten aluminium poured in to cast the down-beam. Every frame casting included a test bar for analysis.

The front forks had been used by Greeves for many years. They were based on short leading links which were joined by a tubular loop that ran behind the front wheel. The link pivots incorporated Metalastic rubber torsion elements to act as the suspension medium, their movement being damped by a pair of Girling units located between the links and the stanchion tubes that

Typical Greeves trials model with alloy down-beam and leading-link forks—in this case, a 1960 Scottish with 9E engine

supported them. These tubes ran up to the headstock where they were joined by top and bottom crowns, the latter welded in place, and the former clamped.

The rest of the frame was more conventional, having a tubular subframe and pivoted rear fork. To hold it all together, and support the engine and gearbox, there was a pair of engine plates. These were bolted to the lower end of the cast-alloy beam, running back to the subframe and rear fork pivot. Normal spring-and-damper units controlled rear wheel movement.

The 1960 range began with three 197 cc models, all powered by the Villiers 9E engine with four-speed gearbox. Two were for trials use and were listed as the 20TC Scottish Trials and 20TCS Scottish Trials Special, the latter having a matt chrome tank and a tuned engine. Otherwise, they were the same, with a saddle, small mudguards set with a large clearance to the 21 in. front and 18 in. rear wheels, and no lights. The last could be supplied as one of several options, including a dualseat, bigger fuel tank and brake drums with light-alloy cooling fins.

The third 197 cc model was announced as the 20SAS, but by the new year it had been replaced by the 20SCS Hawkstone Special, which continued with a more highly-tuned version of the 9E engine. The major changes lay in the frame and cycle parts, for the top tube was bigger and the headstock bosses larger. The latter were to accommodate Timken taper-roller head races instead of the usual ball bearings.

There were other detail improvements, and the rear fork was modified together with the chain line to allow a 4.00 in. section tyre to be fitted. The seat was smaller and lower than before, making it easier for the rider to use a foot when necessary.

The 197 cc models were partnered by 246 cc versions, and the 24SCS also appeared early in 1960. It had the same cycle parts as the 20SCS, but its engine was a modified 33A unit. As well as changes carried out to raise the power output, there were others to strengthen the transmission. These, in turn, allowed the gearbox to run slower, leading to a reduction in rear sprocket size from 70 to 60 teeth. The brake drums with alloy fins were fitted as standard.

Gearbox trouble struck Mike Jackson's 246 cc Greeves during the 1960 100-mile race at Pirbright, so they changed the complete engine/gearbox unit!

Above **The Greeves Sportsman 25DCX with Villiers 2T engine, and odd front-fork spats and headlamp cowl**

Above left **Greeves 24TDS trials model of 1961, with 32A engine—an excellent machine**

Left **The 1962 ISDT Greeves—really the scrambler with an alloy engine top half and road-legal equipment**

There was only one 246 cc trials model, the 24TCS Scottish Trials Special, which was the same as the 197 cc machine except for the 32A engine. This same unit also powered the 24DB Sports model, which was a road machine, so it came with lights, silencer and close-fitting front mudguard. It was equipped with a dualseat, beneath which were the battery, rectifier and tools. These were concealed by a steel pressing, the light switch and horn being set in its front face. Both mudguards were polished light alloy.

The final model in the list was the 25DB Sports Twin, which had a 249 cc Villiers 2T twin-cylinder engine. This was installed in the same set of cycle parts as used for the 24DB and retained the same single silencer fed by a pair of siamezed exhaust pipes. During 1960 it was joined by the 32DB, which differed only in having the 324 cc Villiers 3T twin-cylinder engine.

The 20TC and 20TCS models were dropped during the year, together with many others, and were replaced with improved machines for 1961. As was common practice with Greeves, these kept their basic type number but it was altered by one letter in the suffix to indicate a change. Thus, it was easy to follow the development of the various models from year to year.

For 1961 there were still three 197 cc machines, the 20SCS being continued unchanged. It was joined by the 20TD Scottish Trials model, in which the engine was moved forward and down to help keep the front wheel on the deck during steep climbs. The rear fork pivot was moved forward to keep it close to the gearbox sprocket, but the fork arms were extended to maintain the original wheelbase. A short padded seat replaced the saddle, and a shield was added at a strategic point on the exhaust pipe.

The 20DB Sports Single was a new machine which followed the lines of the existing road models but was fitted with a 9E engine and four-speed gearbox. All the larger models gained taper-roller head races, becoming the 24DC, 25DC and 32DC. The 197 followed suit within a month or so to become the 20DC.

In the 250 class, the trials machine became the 24TDS, being a combination of the 20TD cycle parts and the 32A engine. The 24SCS continued unchanged and was joined by the 24MCS Moto-Cross Special. This was the standard scrambler fitted with a 34A engine that had a Greeves light-alloy head and barrel. An Amal Monobloc supplied the mixture and was fitted with a massive, three-stage air filter developed on the works machines. There were other detail improvements based on Dave Bickers' experiences in the rough and tumble of world-class competition, so the machine represented something close to the optimum in the 250 cc class.

Late in 1961 a small number of ISDT models were built, being based on the 24MCS with the addition of a silencer and lights. Other changes were mainly to suit the machine's specialized purpose, so there was a toolbag on the tank top, more protective front mudguard and competition plates.

For 1962 Greeves followed their usual pattern with not all the changes appearing at once—some models retained their type numbers and others did not. In effect, all models were continued, and the four roadsters (20DC, 24DC, 25DC and 32DC) were the least affected machines in the range.

Of the 197 cc models, the 20TD continued unaltered and the scrambler became the 20SC. The 250s followed suit, with the 24SC and 24TD, but were joined by two new trials models in this capacity. These were the 24TE and 24TES, the former having the 32A engine and the latter the same with the Greeves alloy head and barrel.

Both had a revised frame that continued to have the well-tried Greeves features but was designed exclusively for trials work. Thus, the top tube was curved down to meet the rear of the engine cradle, which was changed from a pair of plates to a welded assembly. The rear fork arms were of rectangular section and there were other detail differences compared to the scrambles frame. The exhaust pipe was run in a loop down in front of the crankcase before being taken up over the right-hand engine cover to the silencer, the tailpipe being tucked neatly inside the rear frame tube.

Early in the year, the new trials frame was used to produce the 20TE model, which had a 9E engine, and at the same time the Moto-Cross Special became the 24MDS. In this form, the machine's engine was developed further to increase its power and installed in a scrambles version of the 24TE frame. There were minor differences, but the rectangular-section rear fork arms and curved top tube were along the same lines. Also new were full-width hubs with light-alloy brake backplates in both wheels, but the brakes themselves remained at 6 in.

A month later, in April 1962, came two further road models based on the existing twins and listed as the 25DCX and 32DCX Sportsman. Engines were the 2T and 3T respectively with twin exhausts and silencers. The frame and forks came from the existing models and were common to both machines, as were all the cycle parts. A new feature was the use of full-width hubs, the front one having an air scoop in the backplate.

The most distinctive features of the DCX models were the front fork spats and the cockpit fairing with its windscreen. Footrests were moved back and up to suit the low bars, and an instrument panel formed part of the fairing. The fuel tank was special, having knee recesses and a quick-action filler cap. In two-tone yellow and light blue, the machine certainly caught the attention.

The ISDT models appeared once again in limited numbers around the middle of the year, following the same lines as before with the alloy top half to the engine. The idea of using a scrambles machine with the minimum of road equipment was most effective.

The 246 cc trials models were altered to follow more divergent paths for 1963, with the 24TES having engine changes and a square-section exhaust pipe. This curled tightly round the left side of the barrel to join a small silencer that was tucked out of the way. The engine cradle was altered with numerous lightening holes, and the seat weight was reduced in part with a fibreglass base. This material was also used for the mudguards. However, some weight was put back on through fitting full-width hubs.

The 24TE went the other way to a simpler and cheaper specification. The tank was changed to a steel version, and light-alloy mudguards were fitted. The engine cradle was replaced by simple, unboxed plates, and the machine lacked the rear chain oiler, competition plate and other refinements to keep its cost down. The 20TE followed its larger brother, as it was the same machine with a different engine.

All the road models continued, with the exception of the 24DC. This still left the customer with the choice of a basic 197 cc machine or a 249 cc or 324 cc twin in DC or DCX trim and finish. These models were joined by two more: the 25DD and 32DD Essex Twins. These were similar to the DC machines, but they had the fibreglass fuel tank and mudguards, fork spats and twin silencers of the DCX. However, the full-width hubs were an option on the DD models.

Of the other models, the 20SC, 20TD, 24SC and 24TD were dropped, but the 24MDS continued unchanged. The 24MD with a 34A Villiers engine replaced the 24SC, using the cycle parts from the 24MDS. It was joined in March 1963 by the 24ME, which had the same set of parts with a 247 cc Villiers Starmaker engine installed in them.

The real news from Greeves for 1963, however, was of their involvement in what was, for them, a new branch of competition, namely road racing. This came about because of the success of a scrambles Greeves in club racing, the machine having been modified in respect of its riding position and tyres. This activity interested Bert Greeves, and the result was the introduction of the 246 cc 24RAS Silverstone late in 1962.

Greeves' announcement came at a time when 250 cc road racing at club level was in the doldrums, with small fields of a very few, expensive, foreign machines and a collection of specials, the latter often cut down from 350s and carrying their weight. The notion of a light, agile two-stroke made sense in terms of performance and cost, and there would soon be a number of such machines on the British scene.

The engine was based on the 24MDS unit with its alloy top half on a 34A lower assembly, but with modified porting to improve the top-end performance. A larger GP carburettor replaced the normal Monobloc and was supplied by a remote, flexibly-mounted float chamber. An expansion-chamber exhaust was fitted, running at high level on the right-hand side. The scrambles gearbox was used with this engine.

The main frame came from the 24MDS, but the subframe was narrowed and the rear fork controlled by a pair of Girling suspension units. The front forks were shortened, and both wheels had full-width hubs but a 19 in. front rim and 18 in. rear. A fibreglass tank and seat pan were fitted, and the controls were adjusted for racing.

That was the prototype, but by the time production began early in 1963, the 24RAS had already been modified. The most obvious changes were to the exhaust system, which ran low down on the left, and the addition of a small head fairing. Further modifications were the use of a 36A engine (but retaining the Greeves parts), a larger GP carburettor and a rev-counter drive taken from the right-hand end of the crankshaft. The gearchange linkage was revised, the front wheel size reduced to 18 in. and the tank altered to provide a well around the single fuel tap.

A limited number of ISDT replicas appeared at the middle of the year once more, and these followed the earlier example by being based on the scrambles model with the addition of some road equipment. Many of the extras were to make the machine suitable for long distances, providing reliability and ensuring quick, easy repairs.

Some Greeves models were available to special order only for 1964. This applied to both DCX models, the 20TE and the 24MD. The road models 20DC, 25DC and 32DC continued, but the 32DD did not. The 25DD remained in the lists for a short time as the MkI, being joined by a MkII, which had the 249 cc 4T Villiers twin engine, a twin-tone horn and a new colour scheme. It retained its fork spats, but the horn and light switches were moved to new locations.

Most of the other models continued with few changes, but while the 24TE stayed the same, the 24TES became the MkII. In this form, its barrel porting was changed to the scrambles layout and a new exhaust system was fitted. The 24ME and 24MDS scramblers were unaltered, but the former was soon dropped, as Greeves preferred to develop their own engine rather than rely on the Villiers A-series or the newer Starmaker.

The first signs of this had been seen earlier in 1963 when a works scrambler had appeared with an Alpha bottom half. The result, early in 1964, was the 24MX1 Challenger, which had an engine with no Villiers parts in it at all. It was still based on the same 66 × 72 mm dimensions, giving 246 cc, but

Above **The 1963 Greeves 24TES with rectangular exhaust, boxed-in and pierced engine plates, and full-width hubs**

Above right **Larger 324 cc Greeves 32DC Sports Twin with the optional finned brake drums**

Right **The 1964 Essex Twin 25DD with spats and styled guards, but lacking the purposeful line of the competition models**

it had an Alpha crankshaft with full-circle flywheels in well-finned Greeves crankcases. The alloy barrel with its iron liner, and the alloy head with curved directional fins, were held down by long sleeve nuts tightened on to studs in the case top. The barrel was square in fin outline, and the inlet flange was not recessed into the fins.

The rest of the engine followed current practice and was robust in construction. An ignition generator was mounted at the right-hand end of the crankshaft with the points, but the coil was external. The gearbox was still an Albion unit, driven by a single-strand chain.

The cycle side was true to form, with the cast-alloy frame beam and leading-link forks. However, it differed in that it lacked an engine cradle, thanks to the inherent strength of the new engine, and

had tubular protection bars under the engine and gearbox, lighter forks and full-width hubs with the fins machined off. The frame was of all-welded construction, not bolted, the rear fork legs were rectangular, and the exhaust was tucked well in on the right, even though the cylinder port was to the left of the frame beam. It was a very functional looking machine.

The same engine went into the Silverstone racer, which became the 24RBS for 1964. In this application, the porting was altered and a larger carburettor fitted, while the expansion box moved to the right-hand side of the machine. The machine also came with a five-speed gearbox, which proved a major headache, as did the clutch. The gearbox problem lay in the Albion design, which moved all the gears on both shafts (except top and bottom) for every change. This meant that in a four-speed box four gears were shifted, but in the five-speed version there were six to move. At racing speeds and power, all too often the six moved past the designated gear into the next neutral. Later on, Greeves offered a four-speed conversion which many riders took up as an improvement. The RBS retained the 6 in. brakes, which were often barely adequate, and during the year a 7 in., twin-leading-shoe option became available, albeit at a price.

Left **The ISDT model for 1964, with Challenger engine and all the right gear**

Below left **Greeves Silverstone road-racing 24RBS of 1964, which served many a novice rider**

Below **The trials 24TFS of 1965, with Challenger top end on a Villiers 32A**

Greeves cut back on the road-going twins at the end of 1964, removing the two DCX models and the 32DC from the list. The 25DD MkII continued, while the 25DC went into MkII form with a 4T engine. The 20DC with its 9E engine remained as before.

On the trials front for 1965, the 246 cc model became the 24TFS, which was powered by a 32A engine with a Challenger top half. The porting remained the same as on the scrambles engine, but the compression ratio was lower, and it had a

Villiers carburettor on a special induction adaptor with an exhaust system to suit. In other respects, the machine was much as before but improved in detail to remove any projections from its underside. The fins were machined from the hubs to reduce weight, the front mudguard was changed to a plastic moulding, and the speedometer to a small round type.

The 24TE with the standard 32A engine remained in the lists together with the 197 cc 20TE. This also applied to the 24MD, 24MDS and 24MX1, but the situation changed early in 1965. All except the 20TE were dropped and replaced by one scrambler: the 24MX2. This had a new design of leading-link forks with curved stanchion tubes and exposed Girling suspension units controlling the pivoted-fork movement. The units provided both suspension medium and damping, so the Metalastic rubbers were dispensed with. Due to their shape, the new forks soon became known as the 'banana' type.

With fork movement increased to over 6 in., the

Left **Greeves 25DD Essex Twin with 4T engine, but without the optional spats in this 1965 picture**

Below left **The 1967 trials 24THS Anglian with 37A bottom half and Challenger top**

Below **Greeves Silverstone in use at Brands Hatch by an aspiring racer under the tuition of the Charles Mortimer Racing School, which ran a whole fleet of these machines**

Greeves 36MX4 Challenger of 1968, with 362 cc engine and twin exhaust pipes

wheelbase was also extended a little, which improved the handling and gave room for a better form of exhaust system. The air filter was improved and so was the gearbox. As a final touch, the colour was changed from the long-running blue to British Racing Green for the frame and forks with pale green for the tank, mudguards and air box.

The road racer became the 24RCS and was fitted with the 7 in. twin-leading-shoe front brake

was a basic machine fitted with the 4T engine. It continued alone for 1966, as the other twins were dropped, but the 20DC Sports Single remained with it. On the competition side, there were only three models; one each for trials, scrambles and road racing.

The trials model became the 24TGS Anglian, adopting the 'banana' forks and a number of weight-saving features. Among these was a much lighter engine cradle, smaller seat and short alloy mudguards. The engine remained the same as for the TFS, but an Amal Monobloc was employed to supply the mixture. The front brake reverted to the older offset pattern, and direct lighting was one of the options available. Colours were light grey for the frame and red for the tank.

The scrambler was the 24MX3 and hardly changed, while the road racer became the 24RDS. The latter had detail changes to the engine and expansion chamber, which made it a faster machine, a new clutch and a much-improved five-speed gearbox. This last item was more compact with a revised gear-selection arrangement and remote pedal pivoted on the right-hand footrest.

Thus, the range was reduced to five models, and of these, the 20DC and then 25DC were dropped during the first half of 1966. The three competition models became the 24THS, 24MX5 and 24RES for 1967, the first two being given the option of Ceriani telescopic forks, made under licence by Greeves, in place of the standard leading-links.

The Anglian showed some detail changes, the base engine becoming the 37A, although the top half remained Greeves with a new exhaust system and an Amal Concentric carburettor. Otherwise, it was much as before, as was the Challenger, which also had the Concentric carburettor and an improved gearbox. The Silverstone entered its final year with some cosmetic alterations, but its best days were over and it had to give way to the six-speed Bultaco and Yamaha twin. For all that, it was still a good club racer with good spares availability and it was not too costly.

The most important news from Greeves for 1967 was their announcement of a second, larger scrambler in the form of the 36MX4 Challenger. This had a 362 cc engine based on the same stroke as the 250 but with a much fatter bore. The barrel was very different, for apart from its size, it also had twin exhaust ports. The pipes from these joined together under the engine to feed into a common expansion chamber.

Otherwise, the design followed the lines of the

as standard together with a full dolphin fairing. The latter had a Perspex bubble over the front competition plate to improve penetration, but this was soon banned by the ACU. There were other detail changes, including a duplex primary chain, but the clutch and gearbox remained problem areas.

In the middle of 1965, the 25DC East Coaster road model was added to the line of twins. This

Above **The 246 cc Greeves Griffon of 1969, with tubular frame and telescopic front forks**

Left **The Anglian trials model in road form, as the 24CS with 'banana' forks, dualseat and lights**

smaller engine and used the same gearbox. The frame was similar to that of the 250, but with duplex seat tubes in place of the usual single item. The 'banana' forks were fitted as standard, with the Ceriani-style versions available as an option. The hubs were conical with 6 in. brakes, the mudguards were light alloy and the fuel tank was in fibreglass. The finish was green with a silver frame.

There were quite a few changes for 1968 plus the addition of a pair of new models, one for road racing and one for trials. The racer came from the logical use of the new bigger engine and was listed as the 35RFS Oulton. This had the scrambles bottom half with the stroke reduced to give the 344 cc capacity. The twin-port barrel remained, but on the racer each fed into a pipe with its own expansion chamber mounted low down on each side. The rest of the machine was the same as the Silverstone, except for a larger tank, but unfortunately the extra power was too much for the frame and brakes. The engine also gave problems.

Further development would have solved these problems, but the costs were too high for Greeves to consider and, as it turned out, any extra effort would have been a waste following the advent of the Yamaha TZ.

Of the existing models, the Silverstone re-mained as the 24RES, and the big scrambler as the 36MX4. The smaller scrambler became the 24MX4 and had a redesigned engine. This was still a 246 cc unit, but it had a short stroke and, therefore, a new crankcase, crankshaft and cylinder. The machine followed the same general lines as its predecessors as regards the engine and gearbox, but it had the same frame as the 360. Both were fitted with the 'banana' forks as standard, with the Ceriani-type an option.

The remaining two models were for trials use, the Anglian becoming the 24TJS. This had REH telescopic forks as standard. It was joined by the 24TJ Wessex model, which retained the 'banana' forks and had a stock Villiers 37A engine, a steel tank and other less costly details to produce a budget model.

It was all change for 1969, only the two scramblers being left in the range but with the new name of Griffon. This was due, in part, to the events at Villiers, but Greeves were less affected than most, as they had progressed to using their own motors. They moved into supplying kit machines in the late 1960s, the two Griffons having the 246 cc engine of the 24MX4 and the 362 cc unit of the 36MX4 bored out 2 mm to give 380 cc.

The engines were fitted with a gearbox designed by Bert Greeves and an all-metal clutch. The bigger version still had twin exhausts, but the expansion box of both models ran above the engine and just below the tank and seat. The frame was new and of all-tubular construction, so it was a real break from Greeves tradition. The front forks were the Ceriani telescopic pattern. Both hubs were conical with 6 in. brakes, being lighter than the old full-width type. Thus, at the close of the decade, the machines became conventional.

In 1970 they were joined by a trials model powered by a 169 cc Puch engine, and later the results of an association with Dr Blair of Queens University, Belfast, were incorporated. The great days were over, but Bert Greeves could look back on the two championships won by Dave Bickers, earlier successes by the great Brian Stonebridge, and hundreds and hundreds of race and trials wins at club level.

Heldun

The small Heldun concern only sold 50 cc machines, and only for a brief period. For all that, the company had a long list of models, but sales were minimal.

The name of the new firm, based in Shropshire, appeared late in 1965. They offered both complete machines and kits for home assembly. The engines were German and Italian and either two- or four-stroke, but there was talk of Heldun producing their own units. These were to have been a twin-cylinder two-stroke and an overhead-camshaft single, but little more was heard of them.

The range catered for most tastes, and for road racing there were the five-speed Hawk and four-speed Hurricane two-strokes. The trials rider was offered the three-speed Husky, which had an ohv engine, high-level exhaust and leading-link forks instead of the telescopics used by the other models.

For road use there were the Harlequin Sports, with a two-stroke, and the Harlequin Supreme, with an ohv engine. Both were available in a de luxe form with dolphin fairing, battery lighting and 60 mph speedometer.

The list was altered for 1967 and, apart from the Hawk racer, all models were fitted with a four-speed gearbox and ohv engine, and were available in kit form only. The range now included a scrambler.

This wide range of models failed to attract many supporters, for 50 cc racing had moved on, 50 cc trials and scrambles were never of interest to competitors, and road users bought basic models or Japanese sports machines. Only the Hunter trials model was mentioned for 1968 before the firm dropped out of sight.

Above **One of the many Heldun machines, on show in Manchester in 1968—only a few were sold**

Left **The Trials Husky with ohv engine, as shown for 1966. Not a success**

Hercules

Although mainly involved with bicycles, in 1960 Hercules decided to try their luck in the moped market. They made no attempt to make their own engine but bought in a 50 cc French Lavalette unit, which had an automatic clutch and single-speed transmission. The drive to the clutch was by V-belt with a chain to the rear wheel, and the drive could be disconnected to allow the machine to be ridden like a bicycle. The engine could be started using the pedals while at rest.

The frame was a simple, rigid arrangement with light, telescopic forks, both wheels having $3\frac{1}{2}$ in. brakes and 23 in. tyres. A large pressing enclosed the space between the engine and the rear wheel spindle, and the rear mudguard had a very deep valance.

For 1961 the brake size went up to 4 in. Unfortunately, the venture cannot have been too successful, as the machine was withdrawn at the end of that year.

The Hercules Corvette in 1960, which had left the market by 1962, with no more impact than it had on arrival

James

Like their group partners, Francis-Barnett, James began to use AMC engines in most of their machines at the beginning of the 1960s. The one exception was the 98 cc Comet, which retained its Villiers engine throughout the production run.

The Comet L1 had either the Villiers 4F or 6F engine, both of which had a two-speed gearbox, but it was controlled by hand on the former and foot on the latter. The complete assembly made a neat and conventional package with a flywheel magneto and direct lighting.

The frame comprised a tubular loop with a pressed-steel centre section that was extended to form the rear mudguard. Telescopic front and pivoted-fork rear suspension was used, and the full-width hubs had a 4 in. brake at the front and a 5 in. version at the rear.

Next in size was the L15A Flying Cadet, which had a 149 cc AMC engine and had been introduced in the autumn of 1959. The engine was the same as that of the Francis-Barnett Plover with three speeds, while the cycle side was similar to the Comet.

There was no 171 cc James to match the Barnett, the next in line being the L20 Captain with 199 cc AMC engine. This was a new machine for 1960. The engine was the same as the Falcon's, but the styling was different, with changes to the tank panels and centre section. The side-panel line was blended in with the deeply-valanced rear mudguard. The tubular frame was conventional, as was the suspension and 5 in. brakes in full-width hubs.

The L25 Commodore with 249 cc AMC engine was similar in appearance, but the rear section of its frame and the mudguard were built up from pressings, so it differed considerably in construction. It also had 6 in. brakes, a deep valance for the front mudguard and a fully-enclosed rear chain.

The range was completed by two competition models, both with the 249 cc AMC engine. For trials there was the L25T Commando, and for scrambles the L25S Cotswold. They had tubular

Above right **James Scooter with its own form of 149 cc AMC engine, having the spark plug right in line with the front wheel**

Right **Superswift M25 of 1962, with Villiers 2T engine and enclosure for the chain and centre section**

Below **James Commodore, which suffered with the 249 cc AMC engine, as did the Francis-Barnett**

Above **James L25T Commando trials model with AMC engine and tucked-in silencer**

Below right **Cadet M15 for 1963—a badge-engineering job based on the F-B Plover 95**

frames and hydraulic front-fork damping, the Cotswold having a Matchless Teledraulic assembly. Fixtures and fittings were appropriate to the machine's use, and included a high-level exhaust pipe and silencer for the trials machine and a stub for the scrambler.

In May 1960 an entirely new model was added to the list. This was the James Scooter, which was powered by a revised version of the 149 cc AMC engine. For this application, the cylinder was horizontal and turned to put the carburettor on the right and exhaust on the left. In this way, it was possible to fit the engine and its three-speed gearbox under the footboard and ahead of the rear wheel, which it drove in the usual manner by chain.

The engine's position meant that it would receive all the dirt and water thrown up by the front wheel, but the addition of a mud-flap dealt with that problem. Another disadvantage was that

it left the plug vulnerable to water from deep puddles. However, it provided better weight distribution and good air flow without a fan or ducting.

The scooter chassis was a duplex arrangement, with tubes from the headstock running down each side of the apron and along the floor sides to the rear. A subframe over the rear wheel supported the seat, and the rear fork pivoted between the main tubes. At the front was a leading-link fork which ran behind the wheel and at its rearmost point was attached to a tension spring and hydraulic damper. Pressings were clipped to the fork arms to improve their appearance, and a large mudguard turned with the wheel.

Both wheels were of the perforated-disc type with 12 in. tyres, and each was located on its hub by six studs. The hubs had 5 in. brakes, the rear version being operated by a pedal on the left. A rocking pedal on the right was used to select the gears, and further back was the kickstart, which was linked to the gearbox by a short length of chain.

The mechanics were enclosed scooter-style with apron, floor, rear section (with access panels) and handlebar shroud. The fuel tank was at the back above the rear wheel, with a good-sized luggage compartment ahead of it under the hinged seat. The battery was in front of this. Engine access was by means of a floor cover.

All told, the James managed to achieve a lighter line than some of its contemporaries, which looked very clumsy alongside the Italian models.

There was a change of colour for some 1961 models, but no other changes until May when the L20S Sports Captain appeared. This was similar to the standard model, but it had a flyscreen, alloy mudguards, 6 in. front brake, much smaller side panels and revised controls. It was a brightly-finished machine aimed at the younger rider.

For 1962 the Comet was only available with the 6F footchange engine unit. Otherwise, the range continued as before, with one addition and a revision to the Commando in line with the experiences of the works team. The new model was the M25 Superswift, which marked a return to the larger Villiers engine. This was the 249 cc 2T twin, and it was installed in the Commodore cycle parts with detail alterations to suit.

There were more changes for 1963, the Flying Cadet and the three models with the 249 cc AMC engine being dropped. The Comet, Captain and Superswift continued with a colour change for the first and last, while the scooter gained a four-speed gearbox, to become the SC4, and the Sports Captain an Italian-style fuel tank.

Four new models were added, the smallest being a new 149 cc Cadet, which was a copy of the Francis-Barnett Plover 95 with its tubular spine frame and humpy tank. For competition use, the Barnett models were also copied, becoming the trials M25T Commando and scrambles M25R Cotswold, both with Villiers 246 cc engines. The former had a 32A unit, and the latter a 36A with Parkinson square-barrel conversion. The machines had a common frame with Norton forks.

The final new model was the M25S Sports Superswift, which combined all the features of the Sports Captain with the Villiers 2T twin engine. It had the same stylish tank, flyscreen and other sporting details.

The basic Superswift was dropped for 1964, but the Sports version continued and was fitted with the Villiers 4T twin-cylinder engine. The rest of the range was unchanged, but only briefly in the case of the M25R Cotswold. In March its engine was replaced by the Villiers Starmaker and it became the M25RS.

The difficult times experienced by the industry restricted James' plans for 1965, so they kept to their existing range, except for the Comet. Although included in the announcement, it was dropped before the new year after a very long run. The scooter went the same way in the middle of

James Cotswold M25RS with Villiers Starmaker engine, as shown at Earls Court late in 1962 and well before it went on sale in early 1964

the year, and at the same time the Cadet was altered to become the M16, matching the Barnett 96. This was a very conventional machine with the three-speed, 149 cc AMC engine unit in a simple loop frame with telescopic front and pivoted-fork rear suspension.

The M16 continued for 1966 together with the Captain, Sports Captain and Sports Superswift for road use, and the competition Commando and Cotswold machines. However, their days were brought to an end in October that year when production ceased due to the problems of the company's parent group. It was a sad end for a firm that had been making motorcycles since Edwardian days.

Norman B3 Sports model, distinguished by the dropped bars and flyscreen from the Roadster

Norman

The small Ashford company of Norman offered both mopeds and motorcycles for 1960, having a total of nine models in its range. All the motorcycles had Villiers engines, as did one of the mopeds.

Each of the three mopeds had a 50 cc engine. They were listed as the Nippy III, Nippy IV and the Super Lido, which had a Sachs engine with two-speed gearbox encased in a streamlined shell. The frame had leading-link front forks and rear suspension, while the improved styling and finish were reflected in a higher price than the Nippy models.

The Nippy III had an Italian Mi-Val engine with single-speed in a rigid frame with leading-link forks. The Nippy IV was similar, but it had a Villiers 3K engine with two-speed gearbox and pivoted-fork rear suspension. Both had a fuel tank that was integral with the pressed-steel frame, and a combined carrier and toolbox over the rear wheel.

The motorcycles were conventional in form, except that all had Armstrong leading-link front forks. The same make of damper unit controlled the pivoted-fork rear suspension, and all models had full-width hubs. The singles were fitted with the 197 cc Villiers 9E engine, the basic model being the B2S with three-speed gearbox. With more comprehensive equipment, it became the de luxe Roadster B2SDL, which offered a choice of three- or four-speeds, deeply-valanced mudguards and rear enclosure panels. This model was also available in Sports form with slimmer and lower bars behind a small screen.

The fourth single was the B2CS competition model with a suitably modified version of the four-speed 9E unit. The frame and cycle parts were altered to suit the machine's use, as were its wheels and tyres.

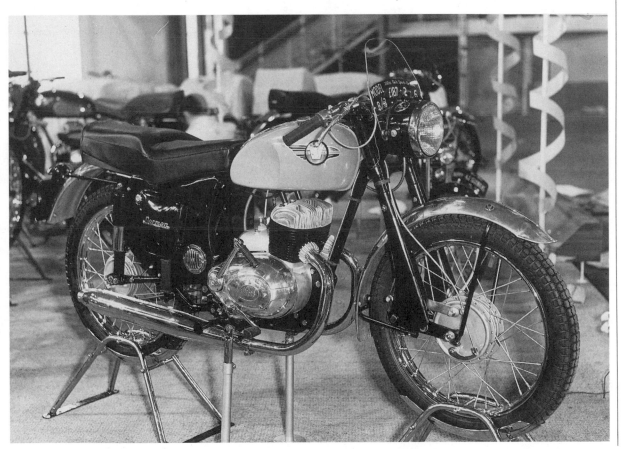

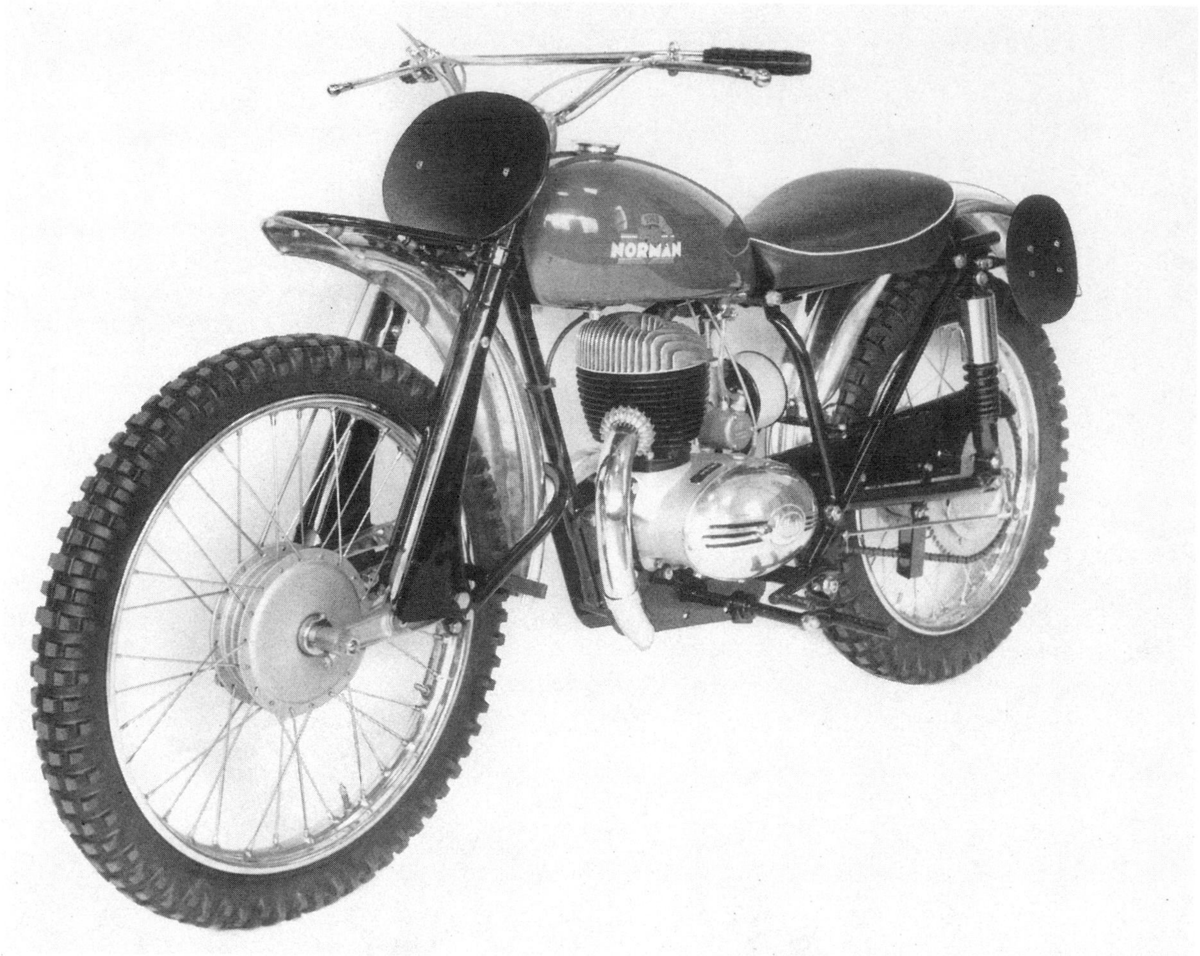
NORMAN

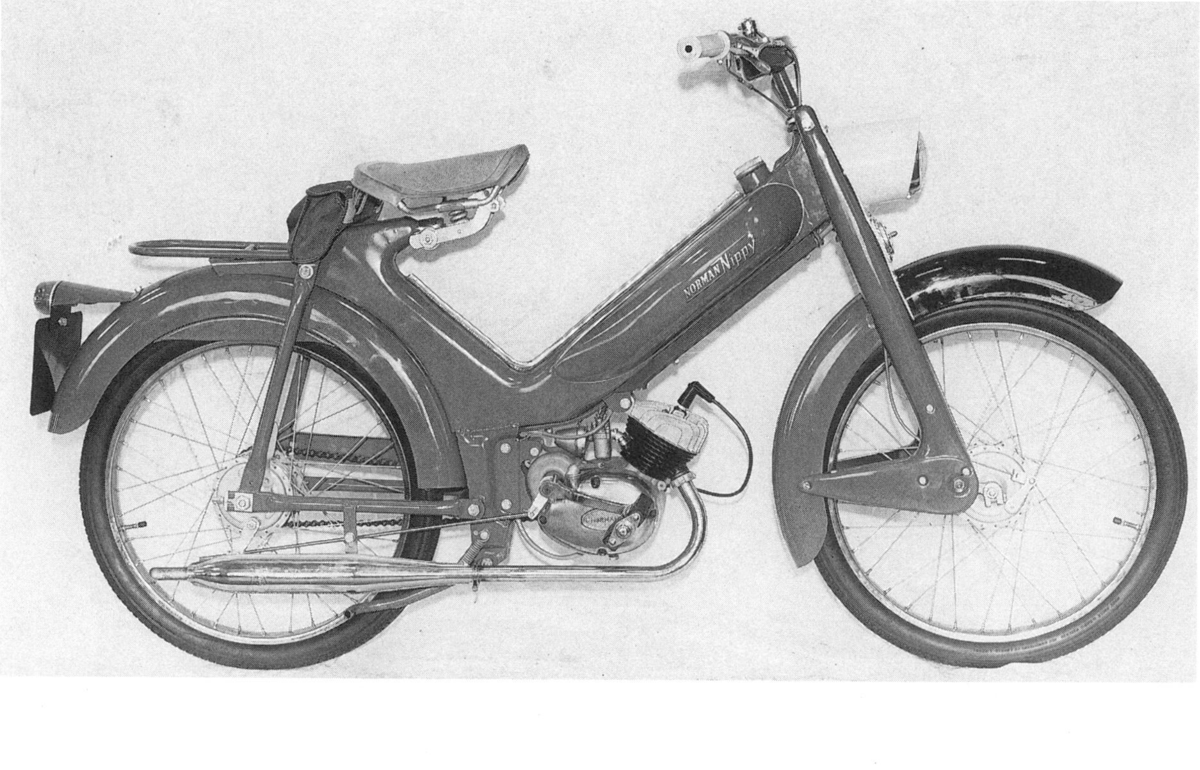
NORMAN Nippy

The final pair of models had the 249 cc Villiers 2T twin-cylinder engine and were listed as the B3 Roadster and Sports. These duplicated the 197 cc model in style and equipment, but they gave a better performance with the bigger engine.

For 1961 the mopeds and 197 cc road models continued unchanged, but there were changes to the twins and competition models. The twins retained the 2T engine but became the B4 Roadster and Sports with a new rear subframe. Both models were given a new Italian-style fuel tank with knee recesses and a quick-release filler cap. The Sports model kept its racy looks, low bars and small screen, while the Roadster had its side panels extended to the rear number plate.

The competition machines became the B4 Trials and B4 Scrambler, the former being available with either the 9E engine or the 246 cc 32A. The scrambler came with the 34A only, and both had the twin's frame with suitable alterations. Footrests were strengthened, an upswept exhaust fitted and a slim fuel tank added, together with alloy mudguards and a small seat.

During 1961 the company moved to Smethwick, having been taken over by Raleigh Industries. This was bad news for riders who liked the Norman machines, for few survived into 1962. All the 197 cc machines were dropped, as were the competition models, leaving mopeds and the two B4 twins.

In fact, the mopeds were now based on Raleigh models. The first was the Nippy V, which had a 50 cc two-stroke engine with V-belt drive and an automatic clutch, but only one gear ratio. Its frame was rigid with telescopic front forks. The second model was the Lido III, which had a similar engine and transmission, but with variable gearing. The suspension was different from the Nippy, with leading-link front and pivoted-fork rear systems.

The Nippy IV with its Villiers engine was also continued into 1962, but only until May. A month later, the B4 Roadster was withdrawn as well. At the end of the year, the Sports twin was dropped, as were the mopeds, bringing Norman production to an end.

Above left **Norman B4C Scrambler for 1961, with 34A engine**

Left **Norman Nippy MkIII of 1961, with Mi-Val engine in nicely-styled rigid frame**

Norton

Norton celebrated the arrival of the decade by introducing rear enclosure on their big twins, following the concept which had appeared on the 249 cc Jubilee twin a year earlier. By then, the single-cylinder range had shrunk to just two road models and two racers, so the company was firmly committed to twins, despite a long history as supporters of the single.

The remaining singles were the well-established 348 cc model 50 and the 490 cc ES2, both with overhead valves and the same set of cycle parts. The two engines were very similar, and their ancestry could be traced back to 1931. They had an unmistakable line that had stayed the same over three decades. The design was very British, with vertically-split crankcase, timing side on the right, iron barrel, alloy head and the ignition control behind the cylinder. The last had been changed to a coil in 1959, so a points housing occupied the space where the mag-dyno had been for so long, and there was an alternator on the left end of the crankshaft in the chaincase.

The four-speed gearbox was the AMC type, based on the old Norton design and fitted by AJS and Matchless as well. The chaincase was the pressed-steel design used by Norton since pre-war days with a slight modification to clear the alternator. The final drive was on the traditional left side, and the chain could be enclosed by an optional case.

The engine and gearbox were separate assemblies held in the frame by plates. Small covers were fitted over these plates to give a smooth look to the package. The frame itself was the famous featherbed in its early wideline form, but with the subframe welded, rather than bolted, in place.

At the front were the equally-famous Roadholder forks, which were available with solo or sidecar yokes and steering dampers. The wheels had full-width alloy hubs, the front with an 8 in. brake and

Above **Norton Navigator 349 cc twin from 1961, in de luxe form with a degree of rear enclosure**

Left **Heave-ho on a 1961 big twin of 596 cc, in de luxe form and with the slimline frame**

the rear with a 7 in. version. The mudguards were valanced and available with an optional chrome-plated finish, while 1960 was one of the years when the road singles were finished in forest green rather than the more usual black and silver. The latter remained an option, however.

The two racing singles were nearing the end of their days, which had begun in 1930 when the Carroll-designed overhead-camshaft engine was first used. Post-war, the Norton racing single became the Manx, and by 1960 was listed as the 348 cc 40M and 497 cc 30M. The engines had received their last obvious external change the year before, when the bottom bevel housing disappeared, but otherwise they showed their 30-year lineage clearly.

The design was simple and sturdy, with a tall crankcase supporting a deeply-spigoted, heavily-finned cylinder. The head was a complex assembly with massive finning and the bevel box bolted to it. This carried the train of gears connecting the two camshafts with the vertical shaft and the cam followers. The bottom end was very rigid with a bevel gear for the cam drive and a spur to the oil pump and the magneto chain, the magneto itself sitting on a platform behind the barrel.

The gearbox was the racing version of the four-speed AMC design, and the three-spring clutch was driven by an exposed chain. The mechanics were fitted in the featherbed frame with Roadholder forks, and the wheels had conical racing hubs with a twin-leading-shoe action at the front. Brake diameters were the same as the road models, but the width was greater. The seat, tank and detail finish were as normal for the Manx Norton.

The rest of the range had twin-cylinder engines, the smallest being the 249 cc Jubilee. This had been introduced late in 1958 and had a unit-construction engine with slightly inclined cylinders, alloy heads with overhead valves, gear-driven camshafts and alternator electrics. The gearbox had four speeds, and the entire assembly was very streamlined in appearance.

It was fitted into a composite frame based on a Francis-Barnett design and built up from pressings and tubes. The front forks came from an AMC lightweight, as did the hubs with their 6 in. brakes. What made the Jubilee different from other Nortons was the extensive rear enclosure, which comprised two side panels and a tail section. The front mudguard was equally extensive, and an optional chaincase was listed to play its part in keeping the works out of sight. To crown it all, there was a new tank style with a long thin badge and two-colour finish.

The major twins were larger, with 497 or 596 cc engines. These were used in machines listed as the 88 and 99 standard or de luxe road models, and the off-road Nomad. The engines were very similar and were based on the Dominator twin, which appeared in 1948. This had a single camshaft at the front of the engine, driven by gears and chain, pushrods in a block tunnel, and a one-piece head and rocker box. By 1960 the last was in light alloy, and the original's dynamo had been replaced by an alternator. Ignition was by coil, except on the Nomad, which retained the magneto. In both cases, the instrument was mounted behind the block where it was chain driven.

The four-speed AMC gearbox was used, and the mechanics of the road models were fitted in the

Above **Norton Atlas scrambler for the USA in 1963, but more an off-road machine with those mudguards and lights**

Above left **Experimental factory Norton in 1961, with low frame and coil ignition—raced by Derek Minter**

Left **The 1962 Atlas with single carburettor and considerable bottom-end power, but the high bars precluded fast riding**

featherbed frame. However, this was not the same as that used by the singles, but a revised design with top rails that were closer together. It was immediately named the slimline. This alteration was the one major change to the welded featherbed frame throughout its life.

The cycle side of the standard twins was the same as that of the singles, but the styling matched that of the Jubilee, with the long, thin tank badge and two-colour finish. The de luxe models also had the same form of rear enclosure as the Jubilee, and this was the reason for altering the frame. The benefits of a narrow seat and a riding position where the rider's legs were tucked in more came as an unsought bonus.

The two Nomad models had tuned engines in the older model 77 frame, which had a single loop with twin tubes under the crankcase and pivoted-fork rear suspension. The machine's equipment was designed for the American enduro market, so it came with lights and a siamezed exhaust system

with single silencer. Other features included a 21 in. front wheel, alloy mudguards and a bright finish.

The Nomads were dropped for 1961, but the rest of the range continued and were joined by new models. The road singles copied the big twins in the use of the slimline frame, adopting the narrower tank, the two-tone styling and a new dualseat. The racing models had a few detail alterations as their production came to an end.

The Jubilee was joined by the 349 cc Navigator, which had a one-piece cylinder casting and increased bore and stroke. To cope with this and the extra power, a forged-steel crankshaft was used, but otherwise the engine unit was basically the same. The gearing was raised to suit the higher road speed and slightly lower engine speed.

The Navigator frame differed in detail, but more obvious was a change to Roadholder forks at the front. Furthermore, these carried the hub and 8 in. brake from the larger machines. These changes altered the front aspect a good deal. The remainder of the machine copied the Jubilee, having the same tank, seat and rear enclosure, but the front mudguard was matched to the forks and wheel, so it had less valancing.

In addition to these two machines, which were listed as de luxe models, there were two standard versions. These came without the rear enclosure and had conventional mudguards front and back. To suit the revised style, the oil tank was moved to the right-hand side and matched by a toolbox on

Left The Norton Jubilee twin in 1964, when it went without the rear enclosure

Above **The last of the Norton model 50 line was this badge-engineered AMC single, which retained the Norton forks and hubs**

Below left **Police Atlas from 1966, with special seat and other equipment for catching the villains**

the left. Small panels blended these items to the seat and the carburettor, although the latter was no longer enclosed.

Of the big twins, the standard and de luxe models, in both 88 and 99 forms, continued as they were, being joined by an enlarged standard model for the American market. This was the 646 cc Manxman, and its extra capacity came from a lengthened stroke. Twin carburettors were fitted, together with a rev-counter drive taken from the end of the camshaft. The bulk of the cycle side was standard featherbed, but the handlebars were of the high-rise type, and the finish less sombre, with chrome mudguards, red seat and polychromatic blue paint.

The Manxman was offered with a number of options, among them a siamezed exhaust, air filter and rear enclosure panels (which called for a single carburettor). Early in the year, the machine took on a European style similar to the other standard twins, although the rev-counter was kept and hung on a bracket beside the headlamp.

Two more twins were announced in April 1961: the 88SS and 99SS sports models. These were based on the standard machines, but they had tuned engines. The extra power came from twin carburettors, bigger ports, a better camshaft and a siamezed exhaust. On the cycle side, flat bars and ball-ended levers were fitted as standard, while the full rear chaincase, rev-counter and rearsets were options.

The road singles continued as they were for 1962, and a few Manx racers were built from spares. For the latter, there were some detail changes to the engine internals, but the most obvious alteration was to the front wheel. This had a new hub with a 7 in. twin-leading-shoe brake on each side.

Most of the twins stayed as they were, but the 88SS was fitted with a downdraught cylinder head. The standard 650 continued and was joined by de luxe and SS versions on the lines of the smaller models, the SS again having a downdraught head. This feature did not appear on the 99SS.

Another bigger twin was announced that year. Known as the 745 cc Atlas, it was listed for export only at first. The capacity was achieved by boring out the 650. Only one carburettor was fitted, together with low-compression pistons. This gave the engine more bottom-end power to suit the chassis style, which was small tank, cowhorn bars, chrome guards and fat tyres.

In the middle of the year, the news broke that the firm was to leave its traditional home at Bracebridge Street and join the AMC group at Woolwich. This decision, and others to rationalize the range, stemmed from the marked drop in sales which had halved in three years to produce trading problems.

As a result, the road singles had a colour change only for 1963, and very few Manx machines were made, bringing their production to an end. It was also the end for the 99 models and the de luxe machines with their rear enclosure.

This left the Jubilee and Navigator in standard or enclosed de luxe forms, and they were joined by one extra model. This was the 383 cc Electra which, on the face of it, was a Navigator with an electric starter. In fact, the changes went deeper, and although the capacity came from boring the 349 cc engine, there were detail changes to accept the fatter barrel spigots and heavier pistons. In addition, the Electra had a different gearbox with a revised selector mechanism.

The special feature of the Electra was its starter motor, which was tucked in behind the block and drove the crankshaft by chain. A second battery increased the system voltage to 12, and another feature was the provision of turn indicators at the ends of the handlebars. The machine had Navigator cycle parts in standard style, but used the 7 in. rear brake from the big twins.

The 88 and 650 continued in standard and SS form together with the Atlas, which was still for export only. It was joined during the year by the Atlas scrambler, which was a combination of the 745 cc engine with twin carburettors and the AMC frame from a CSR. It had the AMC gearbox and alloy primary chaincase, Norton forks and wheels, AMC seat and silencers, and was topped with a tank from a scrambles model.

At the end of the year, the traditional Norton

Below **Norton Atlas for 1968, with humped seat. It was soon to be overtaken by the Commando**

Below right **The Norton P11 hybrid for off-road use, having an Atlas engine in a G85CS Matchless frame with AMC forks and hubs**

Left **Launch Commando in September 1967, minus its badges, but with an eye-catching finish**

Above **Norton Commando S, with camshaft-driven points, at Brands Hatch for a press test in 1969**

Above right **Interpol for apprehending errant drivers, on show at Brighton in 1969**

singles were dropped, as were the de luxe Jubilee and Navigator, and standard 88 and 650 models. In place of the singles came the model 50 Mk2 and the ES2 Mk2, both of which had AMC single engines (as fitted to AJS and Matchless machines) in AMC frames with Roadholder forks and Norton wheels. The machine was the same as that sold under the AMC labels, only the tank badges being changed to suit. The result of this hybrid construction was not to the public taste and sales were poor.

This lack of appreciation of brand loyalty was highlighted further by the use of the Norton Atlas engine in various AMC models, while the Atlas scrambler became the N15CS'N' for 1964 and could become a Matchless with a change of tank badges. That year the Atlas itself was released on to the home market with 12-volt electrics and wider-spaced fork legs to accommodate a fatter tyre. These last two changes also appeared on the

88SS and 650SS, the only big twins left from the many that were in the range only two years before.

Of the small twins, the standard Jubilee and Navigator continued with the Electra, and they ran on into 1965, at the end of which, the two larger models were dropped and the Jubilee had its gearbox replaced by the Electra design.

There were no changes to the singles or twins for 1965 or 1966, but the Jubilee was dropped during the latter year and at the end of it, the two singles and the 88SS also disappeared. It was time for a change, for sales were depressed further and the group was in financial trouble. By the end of

the year, the name had changed to Norton Villiers, and for 1967 the search for a cure to the vibration of the Atlas engine was under way.

While this went on, the featherbed range continued with the 650SS and the Atlas, both using the same set of cycle parts. With them were the N15, which was the Matchless G15 with a Norton tank, and the P11 for off-road use. This retained the Atlas engine, but it was fitted in the G85CS frame with AMC forks and hubs.

Late in 1967 Norton launched their answer to the vibration problem. This was the Commando, and it led to a new range which soon overshadowed the featherbed and hybrid models. Of these, the 650SS and Atlas ran to the end of 1968, and for 1969 the former continued alone as the single-carburettor Mercury. It carried on in this style into 1970 when it was dropped.

The hybrids continued for 1968 without the N15, but with the N15CS, which was based on the older

745 cc off-road models and listed for trail or street scrambler use. The P11 became the P11A and late in the year was renamed the Ranger, but its production ceased at the end of the year, as did that of the N15CS.

To replace this muddle was the Commando, first seen at Earls Court in 1967 and on the road in April 1968. Its engine and gearbox came from the Atlas, but the former was mounted so that the cylinders were inclined forward. They were fed by twin Concentrics. At first, a triplex chain inside a cast-alloy case drove the AMC gearbox through a standard-size plate clutch. However, by the time the machine reached production, this had been changed to one with a diaphragm spring to increase the clamping pressure. This design would be used on all Commando models.

The features that set the Commando apart from other machines were its frame and the way the engine vibration had been isolated from both

The 1970 Norton Production Racing Commando, which was quick

frame and rider. The latter was achieved by mounting the engine, gearbox, rear fork, rear wheel and exhaust system as one complete assembly on rubber insulators. Two main insulators were placed in the mounting plates at the front and rear of the engine and gearbox assembly, while a third was attached to the cylinder-head steady. Others were provided to support the silencers.

The frame had a single, massive top tube with a braced duplex cradle. The rear fork pivoted in the gearbox plates and had no direct contact with the frame. Roadholder front forks were used, and both hubs were the normal Norton full-width, light-alloy types, although the front had a twin-leading-shoe brake fitted as standard.

The styling of the machine was set off by a fibreglass petrol tank and seat tail, which carried the rear light and number plate. The seat itself was also unusual in that its sides were continued forward along the tank to act as kneegrips, side

covers enclosed the centre section of the machine, and just below them were large alloy footrest carriers that helped give it a distinctive appearance.

Late in 1968 the original Commando was joined by the model R, which had a conventional seat and rear mudguard. From March 1969 the former was given the name Fastback and joined by the model S. This had a new engine timing cover that incorporated the points, which were driven from the end of the camshaft. It also had a distinctive style, with small petrol tank, standard seat, rear mudguard and special exhaust system. The last had pipes from both cylinders running at waist level on the left into twin silencers mounted one above the other.

By the autumn the R had been dropped, and the Fastback received the timing-cover points and continued for 1970. The S remained until the middle of that year and was joined in March by the Roadster, which was simply an S model with Fastback exhausts. These two styles of Commando ran on into the 1970s, being joined in time by other models and being fitted with a final enlargement of the engine at 829 cc.

Panther

To most people, the Panther was always a big single with an inclined cylinder that acted as the front down-tube and, as often as not, was seen towing a sidecar. Indeed, that was the case at the beginning and right through to the end, but in between they also produced smaller four-strokes, Villiers-powered lightweights and even a scooter.

The range for 1960 covered all these types, and at the bottom end there were three models with 197 cc Villiers engines. These were the 10/3, which had an 8E engine and three-speed gearbox, the 10/3A, with a 9E and the same number of gears, and the 10/4, which had the four-speed version of the 9E engine.

All had a tubular loop frame with pivoted rear fork, but the one containing the 8E engine differed from the others. At the front, all three machines had a very sleek Earles fork, which looked like a set of telescopics but had the fork pivot to the rear of the mudguard. All models had 18 in. wheels front and rear with full-width hubs and 6 in. brakes. The mudguards were well valanced, and the rear version was blended into a centre enclosure panel below the dualseat. The enclosure contained the electrics and tools, having an access door on each side.

This range of singles was supported by four twins, the smallest of which was the model 35. This had the 249 cc Villiers 2T engine in the same set of cycle parts as the singles, other than the front forks, which were telescopics. There was also the 35 Sports, which had a tuned engine and 7 in. front brake. The 45 Sports had the same brake, but was fitted with the 324 cc Villiers 3T power unit. The 35 Sports also differed from the others in that its rear enclosure was extended to the rear number plate. The same enclosure was used on the model 50 Grand Sports. This had a tuned 3T engine and 8 in.

Panther Grand Sports model 50 of 1960, with the 324 cc 3T Villiers twin engine, at speed on the MIRA track

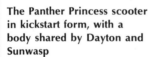

The Panther Princess scooter
in kickstart form, with a
body shared by Dayton and
Sunwasp

brakes at both front and rear.

The rest of the motorcycle range had single-cylinder, overhead-valve engines, the smallest being the 249 cc model 65, which was partnered by the 348 cc model 75. Both had a vertical cylinder on top of a conventional bottom half with the same stroke. A dynamo was mounted on top of the crankcase at the front, while the ignition was at the rear. The 65 had coil ignition with the option of a magneto, but the 75 had the latter as standard. In both machines, the engine oil was carried in a compartment cast into the crankcase, which was a standard Panther feature.

The engine and a separate Burman gearbox were supported in a cradle frame with telescopic front and pivoted-fork rear suspension. The wheels of the 65 had offset hubs with 6 in. brakes, but the 75 had a full-width front hub with a 7 in. brake. This was an option for the 65. The 75 had the same rear hub as the smaller model. Otherwise, the machines followed conventional lines.

The final three motorcycles in the range had the famous Panther 'sloper' engine, which acted as the frame down-tube. The machines were the 594 cc standard 100 and de luxe 100, and the 645 cc 120. The extra capacity came from just one extra millimetre on the bore and six more on the stroke.

There were other differences, but only in detail. They concerned the fixings between the crankcase and cylinder head, which continued on to the headstock. On the model 100, these took the form of two U-bolts, which sat in saddles cast in the crankcase, while on the 120 four long studs were used. Otherwise, it was the same motor with iron head and barrel, enclosed valve gear with single pushrod tube (as on the smaller four-strokes), massive alloy crankcase (which also acted as the oil tank), and a mag-dyno at the top end of the timing side.

A pivoted-fork frame carried both engine and separate gearbox, and there were telescopic forks at the front. The wheels were 19 in. in size, and all the rear ones had full-width, light-alloy hubs with 8 in. brakes. At the front of the standard 100, there was an offset hub with 7 in. brake, but the other two models had a front brake and hub to match the rear, the two being interchangeable. One

Above **The big 'Pussy' model 120 Panther, with 645 cc single-cylinder engine doubling as the down-tube, as always**

Below **Panther 35 with 2T engine in 1961**

further difference was that these two had twin-port cylinder heads and two exhaust systems, while the standard 100 only had a single exhaust port and system.

The mudguards were well valanced, and all models had a dualseat. There was some variation in finish to distinguish them. As most were destined to haul a sidecar, all were supplied with gear ratios to suit, but solo gears were available to order.

That completed the motorcycle range, but for 1960 it was joined by a scooter, which was available in two versions. This was the Princess and was listed as the 173KS and 173ES with kick and electric starting respectively. Earlier, Panther had imported the French Terrot scooter, but this had not sold very well. However, it led to their own design, which was first seen late in 1958, reaching the market a year or so later.

The bodywork and the massive backbone tube of the main frame had much in common with the Dayton Flamenco and Sunwasp, as they had shared the tooling to reduce costs. Differences centred on the front mudguard, apron and details of design.

The Princess was powered by a 174 cc Villiers 2L engine with fan cooling and either a flywheel magneto or a 12-volt Siba Dynastart. Both models had a four-speed gearbox, and in the kickstart version the pedal shaft was linked to the gearbox by a short chain and two sprockets. Gear changing was by heel and toe pedals on the right side of the floor, while the footbrake was on the left.

The frame followed normal scooter practice with a large backbone tube and rear subframe. Both front and rear suspensions comprised a pivoted arm controlled by a single spring-and-damper unit on the left. The wheels were 10 in. split-disc types and were fitted to light-alloy hubs with 6 in. brakes.

The bodywork was in the usual style, with apron, floor, rear body and detachable side panels. The front mudguard was fixed, and there was a hinged dualseat, beneath which was the fuel tank. There were twin glove boxes in the rear of the apron and a fascia panel for the instruments, switches, and ignition and neutral warning lights.

Both scooters continued for 1961, but among the motorcycles the 10/3, the standard 35 and the ohv 65 were dropped. This left the 10/3A and 10/4 with 9E engines, the 35 Sports with the 2T engine and the two models with the 3T engine. The four-strokes also continued as the 75, the 100 (in

Big single, plus sidecar, being checked over in 1961, when its role had been taken over by the Mini. Note the riding gear from an earlier period

Above right **The 1963 Panther single in pivoted-fork frame, but still with twin exhausts**

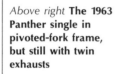

Right **Panther 35ES for 1966, with neat flyscreen, but still with the older 2T Villiers engine, which was topped by a nice tank**

standard and de luxe forms) and the 120.

All except the 75 remained for 1962, when two more versions of the scooter were added to the lists by fitting the 197 cc 9E engine with kick or electric starting. However, it was not a good time for the company, as the market in general was contracting and nowhere more so than with sidecars, which fell victim to the Mini. This was a major blow to Panther, and the firm had to call in the Official Receiver late in 1962. After this, motorcycle production declined and they took on more general engineering work.

The effect was to reduce the range considerably for 1963, only five models being left. There was one scooter, the 173KS, no two-stroke singles but two twins. These were the 35, which returned to the range with telescopic forks, rear enclosure and a 7 in. front brake, and the 45 Sports which was

unchanged. The big four-strokes were reduced to the de luxe 100 and the 120, both of which were experiencing supply problems with their Burman gearboxes and Lucas mag-dynos, since the makers of these considered them obsolete. However, enough stocks were gathered together to keep production going at a low rate.

For 1964 the range was reduced further, the Princess scooter and standard model 100 being dropped. A year later the 45 Sports was discontinued, and the big single became the 120 de luxe. The 35 was given electric starting for 1966, but by then some of its parts were being brought in from component suppliers and were common to other makes. In this manner, the 35 and 120 models trickled on until 1968, when production finally ceased.

Phillips

One of the Raleigh group of companies, Phillips produced their own small range of 50 cc mopeds from 1959 onwards. There were three for 1960, two with Rex engines and the third with a Villiers 3K unit and two-speed gearbox. This model was the P45 Gadabout, which had a spine beam frame, telescopic front forks and full-width hubs. Standard equipment included direct lighting, a saddle bag, twistgrip gear-change and rear carrier.

The P50 Gadabout de luxe had a Rex engine with three-speed gearbox, but otherwise was the same. Its twistgrip gear-change was designed to stop the rider missing the middle ratio, but a trigger allowed direct top-to-bottom changes in either direction.

The third model was the P40 Panda, which had a single-speed Rex engine in a cycle frame and forks, providing basic transport. During 1960 it was joined by the P49 Panda Plus, which had telescopic front forks and deeply valanced mudguards.

The Phillips P49 Panda Plus of 1960, posed in a park with a model recruited from the staff

Above **Phillips P50 Gadabout in another pose at the Birmingham municipal golf course offices**

The P40 was dropped at the end of the year, but the other three models remained for 1961. The P49 was discontinued at the end of that year, but the P45 and P50 continued for 1962 and were joined by two new models. These were both based on Raleigh machines which, in turn, were made under licence from Motobécane in France. One was the PM1 Panda MkIII, which had the engine, automatic clutch and single-speed transmission slung from a rigid spine frame with telescopic front forks. The PM2 Gadabout MkIV had automatic variable gearing plus pivoted-fork rear suspension and a dualseat.

The P45 and P50 were dropped at the end of 1962, but the two PM models continued for a year or so. Then Raleigh dropped the Phillips moped brand and concentrated on their own marque.

Right **Phoenix scooter, listed as the T250, with 2T Villiers engine**

Phoenix

Phoenix, the name of a mythical bird that arose from its own ashes, was first used on a trio of road-racing machines built by Ernie Barrett in the early 1950s. All had JAP engines and similar chassis with a duplex frame, long leading-link front forks and pivoted-fork rear suspension.

The engines were singles of 250, 350 and 500 cc, giving Ernie three rides at each race meeting and the advantage of spare frames by switching units around. In practice, it was rather too much for one man with limited assistance, and a common sight in race paddocks of the period was Ernie feverishly working on one machine and then rushing out on another for practice or a heat.

So Ernie turned to another venture, which was a scooter built in his small Tottenham works and launched for 1957. By 1960 he had quite a range, all fitted with Villiers engines and based on the same set of cycle parts. Each of the singles was listed in more than one version to augment the numbers and give the customer more choice.

The tubular frame extended to the tail of the machine, and there was a sheet-metal floor that was continued at the front as the apron. The engine assembly was just ahead of the rear wheel and had a simple shield over it to keep road dirt at bay. The wheel was suspended in a pivoted fork, and its movements were controlled by twin spring units installed beneath the scooter's floor. They were connected to drop arms from the rear fork.

The front suspension comprised a single pivoted arm controlled by one spring unit. The wheels were pressed discs with an 8 in. diameter for Standard models and a 10 in. size for the rest, the latter being an option for the basic machine. The hubs contained 5 in. brakes.

The basic chassis carried a plastic body. At the front, one large moulding was fixed to the apron to form the front mudguard, headlight and horn mounting. Behind the apron was a glove box with the speedometer and light switch in its top face. At the rear was another large moulding that incorporated the fuel tank. It was held by quick-release catches, and its removal gave excellent access to the mechanics.

A large dualseat on top of the rear body was

hinged at one side to give access to the fuel filler cap and the sparking plugs. Other detail features included a good prop-stand on each side of the machine, a positive-stop gear-change pedal and a neutral finder, which worked from first or second gears.

The smallest model was the 147 cc Standard 150, which was fitted with a Villiers 30C engine and three-speed gearbox, kickstart and fan cooling. Next came the Super de luxe 150, which differed in having a 148 cc Villiers 31C engine, four speeds and battery lighting. Finally, there was the S150, which had the 31C engine, but only three speeds. However, it was equipped with Siba electric starting.

The next two classes of machine were very similar, and the smaller of the two had the 174 cc Villiers 2L engine in the same three models with the same numbers of gears and Siba electric start. The larger version had the 197 cc 9E engine in the three models with a change to four speeds only for the S200 with its electric start.

The final pair of machines had twin-cylinder engines and were listed as the T250 and T325. Both had fan-cooled Villiers power units with Siba electric start and a four-speed gearbox. The former

had the 249 cc 2T engine, and the latter the 324 cc 3T unit.

For 1961 the range continued with one major alteration. The front mudguard moulding was extended to include the apron, and at the same time the large glove box was made even bigger, while the handlebar cover was revised. The trend was continued for 1962, when the floor became part of the body and front moulding, and the pivoted rear fork was controlled by a single, hydraulically-damped spring unit.

There were more changes for 1963, a cheaper pair of twins being introduced as the Super de luxe 250 and 325. Both had a lot in common with the existing models, but they lacked electric starting and fan cooling. They were fitted with the basic 2T and 3T engines.

The rest of the range stayed, except for the Standard 150, which was replaced by a newcomer. This was the Standard 100, which was the same as the others but had a 98 cc Villiers engine with two-speed gearbox. It had 8 in. wheels and a smaller fuel tank.

There were no changes for 1964, but in a contracting market-place there was little room for the small firm, and the make faded from the scene.

Phoenix T250 with the rear body removed to show the ducting of the fan-cooled, electric-start Villiers twin

Radco

For a while in the late 1960s there was a move (mainly in the USA) to mini-bikes, which were crude, simple machines that were easy to sling in the back of a car or pick-up. Most were American or European in origin, but the Radco, which made a brief appearance in 1966, hailed from Britain.

The company name was an old and respected one, dating back to just before World War 1, and it had enjoyed its best days in the 1920s. Radco produced motorcycles until 1933, but then turned to component manufacture. During the 1950s a machine was announced, but the firm had second thoughts and it did not reach production.

Then, late in 1966, they displayed the Radco-muter at the Earls Court Show. This was a very basic mini-bike which was powered by a 75 cc Villiers lawn-mower engine with side valves, single speed, automatic clutch and pull-cord starting. The engine was clamped into a simple, rigid duplex frame, which had rigid forks at the front, 'doughnut' tyres, and the seat and tank laid on the twin top tubes. Controls were minimal, there were no lights, and there was a brake for each wheel—both operated by hand.

The machine could be carried easily in a car boot, but it failed to raise much interest. No more was heard of it, and the firm went back to component making.

The Radco of the 1950s, which was basic, but the Radcomuter was even more so

Raleigh

The Raleigh company has always been known for its bicycles, but it was involved with powered machines as far back as the Victorian era. They returned to this field after World War 1 and also sold engines and gearboxes to other firms under the Sturmey-Archer label.

The machines remained in production until 1933, after which the firm turned to three-wheel cars and vans, which they had begun working with in 1930. In 1935 this activity also stopped and they concentrated on bicycles only for over two decades. Late in 1958 they reappeared on the motorcycle scene with a moped, as this tied in well with their existing business, being a natural progression for many of their customers.

Raleigh's moped had a simple Sturmey-Archer two-stroke engine with overhung crankshaft and cast-iron cylinder. A Lucas flywheel magneto was mounted at the left-hand end of the crankshaft, and a V-belt ran between this and the crankcase to drive a countershaft. This, in turn, drove the rear wheel by chain, which could be disconnected if necessary. The normal pedal chain was retained, and the engine assembly was hung from two lugs on the frame, being isolated with rubber bushes. The engine was made for Raleigh by the BSA group.

The frame was basically that of a woman's bicycle with suitable strengthening, rigid forks and no rear suspension. The fuel tank was mounted between the two down-tubes, and a two-piece shield partly enclosed the engine, running back to cover the drive chains. The controls were of the simplest, with the twistgrip working both throttle and decompressor. It was the only control, other than the two brake levers.

Soon, the company offered such options as a screen, legshields and panniers, and during 1959 a second model with a clutch was introduced. This device was built into the countershaft belt pulley and was controlled by a further handlebar lever, which could be clipped into the 'clutch out' position to make the machine easy to handle when the engine was not running.

The Raleigh moped at its launch, late in 1958, at the Savoy Hotel in London. On the left is cycle champion Reg Harris, flanked by the firm's chairman and Sir Leslie Robinson of the Board of Trade

The Raleigh Roma scooter of Italian origin, as seen in 1961

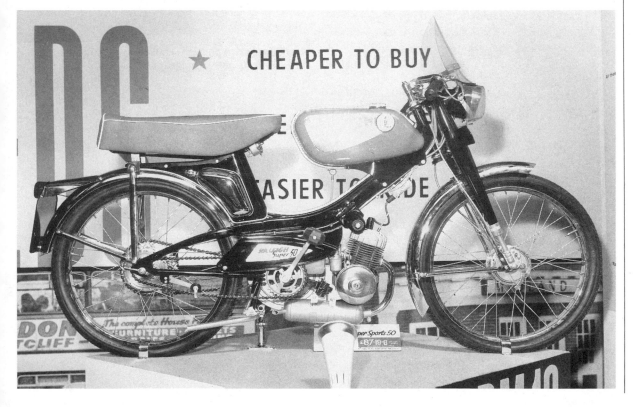

Below **Raleigh RM12 sports moped of 1965, with neat bars and screen above, but distinctly standard parts below**

CHEAPER TO BUY

Above **Raleigh RM8 Automatic MkIII of 1964, with its Mobylette engine that superseded the original Sturmey-Archer**

Right **The 1965 RM5 Supermatic with variable-ratio belt primary drive and short leading-link forks**

For 1960 only the model with the clutch was offered, and it was in a revised form, being listed as the RM2C. The fuel tank had been enlarged, the gearing lowered, the silencer improved, and a fairing fitted to the down-tube to flow into the line of the tank.

At the end of the year Raleigh changed their tactics, replacing their own moped with one built as a copy of the French Mobylette under an agreement with Motobécane. In addition, they decided to venture into the scooter market and came to an arrangement with Bianchi of Italy to market the Orsetto model under the name Roma. In time, this was built under licence by Raleigh.

The mopeds were the RM4 and RM5. Each had a 50 cc two-stroke engine, and the former was named the Automatic. It had a single speed, automatic clutch, rigid frame and telescopic forks. The brakes were small, and the lighting direct. The latter model was called the Supermatic and had an automatic, variable-ratio primary belt drive. This machine had a frame with pivoted-fork rear suspension and leading-link front forks. The lighting remained direct, and it had a dualseat.

The Roma scooter had a single-cylinder 78 cc

engine, which lay beneath the central enclosure panels as a result of its horizontal cylinder. This was in cast-iron with a light-alloy head, the parts being fitted to a crankcase that extended back to include the gearbox. The electrics were on the left of the crankshaft, and the helical-gear primary drive on the right. The three-speed gearbox was of the all-indirect, cross-over drive type, so the final-drive chain was on the left where it was fully enclosed.

The frame was based on a single main tube welded to a subframe at the rear, which supported the dualseat and the fuel tank beneath it. Rear suspension was by pivoted fork, which was controlled by a pair of units that employed rubber discs as the suspension medium. Thus, they were quiet in use and maintenance free. A similar pair

Raleigh RM7 Wisp finished with 'diamond' studs for show at Earls Court in 1967

was used at the front to control short trailing links. Both wheels had light-alloy, split-disc rims with 8 in. diameter tyres and 5 in. brakes.

The bodywork followed normal scooter lines, with a tunnel in the floor for the engine, and footboards to each side. These last were moulded in reinforced plastic, the same material being used for a luggage well behind the fuel tank and the rear chaincase. The main body, central engine cover, front mudguard and apron were steel pressings.

The three machines continued in this form for 1962, and only the scooter was changed for 1963. It became the MkII with a little more power from engine revisions, lower-ratio but more robust gearing, and some more plastic panels and parts. It entered 1964 in this form, but during the year it was modified in detail to become the MkIII. A few of these models had a light-alloy barrel in place of the usual iron version, but the machine was dropped at the end of the year.

The moped range remained, and during 1963 it was extended by the RM6 Runabout. This was similar to the RM4, but it had cycle-type forks and the fuel tank was above the rear wheel. It kept the single speed, automatic clutch and spine frame. The brakes comprised a full-width drum hub at the rear and a caliper type at the front.

The RM4 was dropped early in 1964, leaving the RM5 and RM6, which were joined by the RM8 Automatic MkI. This was similar to the RM6, but it had a telescopic front fork with a full-width hub and drum brake. Later that year the RM9 Ultramatic was introduced. This was similar to the

RM8, but with the variable gear ratio of the RM5.

All four models continued for 1965, and during that year they were joined by two more. One was a de luxe version of the RM6 with a better engine and other improvements; the other was the RM12 Super 50. This was a sports moped built on motorcycle lines, but it retained the automatic clutch and variable gear ratios. It had a rigid frame with telescopic forks and small drum brakes. During the year the RM5 was also given telescopic front forks.

The six machines remained for 1966, and a newcomer was added. This was the RM11 Super Tourist, which was a touring version of the RM12. All went forward for 1967. This year saw the introduction of the Pop model, which was a cheaper version of the RM6 finished in black, but it was dropped within a few months. A second new model was the RM9 Ultramatic Plus One, which was the standard model with reinforced rear wheel, dualseat and pillion rests.

During 1967 a new style of moped appeared with the usual single-speed engine unit. It was the RM7 Wisp. The use of 12 in. wheels followed a trend in the bicycle world, and the layout, styling and frame design were suitably modified. The frame remained rigid, as did the forks, and the machine had drum brakes, direct lights and a cylindrical fuel tank, which was tucked in behind the seat tube under the saddle.

Later in 1967 the RM11 and RM12 were dropped, but the remaining seven models continued until late in 1969 when production ceased.

Rickman

Derek and Don Rickman's story is one of brilliant riding and successful endeavour. They began in trials but progressed to scrambles, gaining innumerable wins at national and international level. With such experience, they became disillusioned with the standard scramblers they were riding and decided to do something about it.

The result appeared in 1959 and was the first Tribsa, a name given to any amalgamation of Triumph engine and BSA frame. The Rickmans used Norton forks for their machines, as they flexed less than AMC ones, and the engines were pre-unit Tiger 100s, specially tuned for scrambles use. The wheels and gearbox were BSA parts, and there were a number of minor detail improvements to the cycle parts.

The machine was called the Metisse, which is French for a female mongrel—the brothers preferred it to the male *metis*. The machines were built to a very high standard, and a typical example of the care taken in their construction was demonstrated by the engine bolts. These were close-tolerance aircraft components, which were

The fabulous Rickman Metisse in October 1960, shown here with Richard Wyler, who starred in the Man from Interpol **TV series, between races on a Greeves**

a press-fit in new light-alloy engine plates, so the assembly contributed to the overall stiffness of the frame.

The brothers were very successful with their new machines and, inevitably, the Tribsa idea was copied by many, although few were built to the same high standards. For 1960 a fibreglass tail-cum-side-panel unit was added and developed further during the year by Doug Mitchenall. Later, he joined the brothers, and together they designed and made the fuel tank, seat pan, rear mudguard, front mudguard, side panels (which acted as competition plates) and air filter, all of which fitted together in one sleek assembly.

There was a continual demand for the machines, but the Rickmans found themselves in hot water. The industry did not take kindly to a motorcycle dealer using their components and consistently beating them with the end product. Nor did they like the fact that customers flocked away from their models to those of the Rickmans, particularly as the market was in decline.

Suddenly, engines, gearboxes, frames and even spares were out of stock to the brothers, but this simply made them more determined. If they could

not buy, they would make, and so was born the first Rickman rolling chassis and a new standard was set.

The frame was a duplex type, bronze welded from Reynolds 531 tubing and finished in bright nickel plate. It was light, well braced and a classic. The rear fork was made in the same manner, with a fixed mounting for the wheel and eccentric adjusters at the pivot point to set the chain tension.

They also made the front forks, which had internal springs and sealed damper units, but the early wheel hubs came from the British Hub firm. Later, they made their own conical hubs, first in alloy and then in magnesium. The tank, seat base, mudguards and centre panels continued in fibreglass, and the footrests were in tempered steel. The engine plates were made originally to suit a pre-unit Triumph engine.

Don Rickman used one of these machines to such good effect that he was third in the 500 cc World Championship, despite missing some rounds. The result was inevitable—a flood of orders for replicas, but before taking these up the brothers offered their design to any British

Above right **Unusual combination of a Velocette engine in a Metisse frame, but built to the usual high standard around 1968**

Right **Rickman Metisse fitted with Royal Enfield Series II Interceptor engine. Disc brakes were unusual at the front, and very rare at the rear in 1970**

Left **This model is on show at Earls Court late in 1966, when Rickman had an involvement with Bultaco**

The Rickmans' immaculate glory, housing a Triumph engine in their own set of café-racer parts

manufacturer who might wish to use it. They were met with a stony silence so, rather reluctantly, they became motorcycle builders. To avoid some of the previous supply problems and also purchase tax, they built frame kits and modified the engine plates to suit a range of engines and gearboxes. It was then left to the customer to find his engine and prepare it as he wished.

Around 1963 they finally secured a supply of engines from AMC and were able to offer these with the kits. Derek used one to win the 750 cc European title. In this form, the brothers' machines

continued to be in great demand, but looking to the future, they began to introduce other lines.

One new idea was a smaller scrambles kit, which was for use with BSA or Triumph unit-construction engines. Another was a move into road racing, one outcome being the Dresda Metisse, which combined their frame with a Triumph engine prepared by Dave Degens, who normally built Tritons. From these experiences came a street kit, but prior to this they produced another frame to suit a smaller, two-stroke engine.

Early in 1964 there was a tie-up with Bultaco to produce frames for the 250 cc Spanish engine and to import the marque. This was developed, and at the end of the year the Bultaco-Metisse scrambler appeared as a complete machine. It was just like the larger models, but scaled down to suit the smaller engine. It had Bultaco forks and hubs.

The arrangement with Bultaco continued for a period, but then the Spanish company went elsewhere. This left a vacant set of cycle parts, which were fitted with various engine units, including the Villiers Starmaker until the supply dried up. Then, they moved to a German Zundapp unit, and later still a Montesa. An association with Weslake in the late 1960s led to the Rickmans marketing an eight-valve conversion for the big Triumph twin. Unfortunately, this came too late, for the trend was toward the new superbikes, and it was too early for the classic revival that was to occur in the 1980s.

Consequently, the Rickmans moved into fairings, top boxes and panniers, and soon found themselves well occupied in the boom years of the 1970s. But they never forgot their roots or their high standards, which continued to set the pace among any range of accessories. The lovely frame kits continued too, being modified to take the big four-cylinder engines from Japan.

Royal Enfield

The Enfield range for 1960 comprised a dozen models, and in typical fashion it covered the market well. There was a small two-stroke, a full range of four-stroke singles (including a competition model) and four twins. As was normal with the marque, these machines shared many common parts and, as the decade progressed, more new models would be produced by ringing the changes with standard assemblies.

The two-stroke was the 148 cc Prince, which was the final version of a design that could be traced back to 1939 and which had served in the war. It had been developed over the years, and by 1960 emerged as an up-to-date machine. The engine was built in unit with the three-speed gearbox and, when fitted to the Prince, had full flywheels. Its construction was conventional in most aspects, but it differed from its contemporaries in having the clutch on the left-hand end of the crankshaft and the generator on the right. More usual were the alloy head, iron barrel and four main bearings.

The Prince had a simple loop cradle frame with pivoted-fork rear suspension. Telescopic forks were fitted at the front, and both wheels had full-width hubs with 5 in. brakes. The rear chain was on the right, as the gearbox was of the cross-over design, and a very extensive rear chaincase was provided. The mudguards were well valanced, and the area beneath the dualseat was enclosed by side covers. The fuel tank held 3 gallons of petrol, which was an increase on the earlier model.

As with the rest of the range, the Prince was available from the factory with a dolphin fairing. This was called the Airflow, and it came with moulded-in storage pockets and a screen. The

Royal Enfield Continental GT of 1965—a factory-built café racer with ALL the goodies demanded by young riders of that period

1960 Royal Enfield 499 cc Bullet, which had a long pedigree

Prince version differed from the others in size, but all followed the same lines.

The fairing option had its roots in 1956 when the factory had co-operated with *The Motor Cycle* to build the Dreamliner fairing on a 346 cc Bullet model. It had been a futuristic design with full front and rear enclosure and twin headlights, which had proved most successful. Royal Enfield had thought that the design was too radical and too expensive for the public, but they went on to produce the Airflow type in 1958. By 1959 it was available for all their models.

The next three machines in the range were based on the same 248 cc single-cylinder four-stroke engine. This was the Crusader, which had appeared in 1956 and was of unit construction with some features which did not follow the standard English pattern. For all that, it was a neat package, with the mechanical parts enclosed in castings to make one smooth assembly.

Although the Crusader began life with an iron cylinder head, by 1960 this was cast in light alloy. However, the barrel remained ferrous. Unusually, the crankshaft was also in cast-iron and, since it was in one piece, the connecting rod had a split big end and shell bearings. The alternator was at the right-hand end of the crankshaft, while the timing gear and oil pumps were on the left—the opposite of normal British practice.

The valve gear was simple, with a chain-driven camshaft, the followers and pushrods moving in a tunnel cast in the cylinder barrel. The camshaft drove the oil-pump gears, the lubrication system being dry sump, although the oil was carried in a chamber that was integral with the crankcase in typical Enfield fashion. A shaft ran across the engine from the front timing gear to the ignition points cam and its advance mechanism on the right.

The four-speed gearbox followed normal lines and had its own oil supply. Its output sprocket was on the left, inboard of the clutch, and the castings were designed to form the front end of the full chain enclosure. The chain emerged from rear-facing ports in the castings, and its runs passed through flexible gaiters to the rear wheel. The kickstarter and gear-change pedals were on the right.

The engine unit was installed in an open frame with single top and down-tubes plus a duplex subframe. Suspension was by telescopic front and pivoted rear fork, and both wheels were 17 in. diameter with full-width hubs and 6 in. brakes. At the top of the front forks was the Enfield casquette, a housing for the headlamp, speedometer and light switch with twin pilot lights set in it near the top. As lights, they were of no real use, but they met a legal requirement.

The Crusader had a good pair of mudguards, a 3-gallon petrol tank and a dualseat. Under the seat's nose was an assembly that combined several features into one. It carried the air cleaner,

Above **1961 Royal Enfield Prince with Airflow fairing at Earls Court**

Below **The 1961 Meteor Minor Sports of 496 cc, with low bars and siamezed exhaust system**

Above **Royal Enfield Crusader, of 1961, was the basic 250 model for learners and commuting**

Below **346 cc Clipper, which combined the Bullet engine with the Crusader frame. It is shown here in its 1961 form and finish**

The 1962 Super Meteor with a degree of enclosure for the rear half

ignition switch, battery, toolkit and the rectifier, with a lid on each side for access. Legshields were available as an option, and by 1960 so was an Airflow fairing.

Built in this form for 1960, the Crusader was listed with the Clipper II and Crusader Sports models. The former was an economy version, which achieved its lower price by having a chainguard in place of the full chaincase, a saddle rather than a dualseat, an offset rear hub and fewer polished engine castings.

The Crusader Sports went the other way, with raised compression ratio, larger Amal Monobloc, bigger inlet valve and hotter cams to raise the power output. It had a 7 in. front brake, larger fuel tank and sports handlebars.

Next in the range were three 346 cc models and a 499 cc machine. All were single-cylinder four-strokes based on the sporting Bullet range, the name of which dated back to 1933. In 1948 the name had been revived for a series of machines characterized by having the oil tank cast as part of the crankcase and the gearbox bolted to the back of the engine.

In other ways, the construction was conventional, the timing arrangement and oil pumps being on the right. The former comprised a train of gears which ran from the crankshaft to the rear of the engine, where they drove the points of the coil-ignition system. The plunger-type oil pumps were driven from the crankshaft by a shaft in the timing cover, beneath which was an oil filter.

The crankshaft was built up, but it had a plain-bush big-end. The barrel was cast in iron with tunnels for the pushrods, while the head was in light alloy. The crankcase casting extended back to form the oil tank as a separate compartment, and its rear face provided the gearbox mounting. Carburation was by Amal, and an alternator was mounted on the left in the primary chaincase.

The gearbox had four speeds, and its gear pedal and kickstart lever were on concentric shafts. It featured the much-publicized 'neutral finder', which was a small lever mounted above the others. When pressed, it would select neutral from any gear except first.

This form of semi-unit engine and gearbox construction was fitted to the 346 cc Bullet model G2 and the 499 cc Bullet model JS. Both had an open frame, telescopic front forks and pivoted-fork rear suspension—all very similar to the Crusader. The same designs of front fork casquette, deep tank, dualseat and centre section were used, and some parts were the same. Wheels were 17 in. for the G2 and 19 in. for the JS, with 7 in. brakes for the former and the rear of the latter. The front of the JS had dual 6 in. drums to give balanced braking.

In addition to the standard Bullets, there were two other models of similar form, both with 346 cc engines. One was the 350 Clipper, which had begun life with a separate gearbox, but for 1960 became a cheaper version of the Bullet. As such, it was very similar, but it managed with a single 6 in. brake at the front.

The second model differed rather more, being

the Works Replica Trials, which had an all-alloy engine, magneto ignition, special heavy flywheels and a small-bore carburettor. The exhaust system was raised and the gearing lowered.

Cycle parts were altered to suit trials use, but they remained in the style of the standard model. Thus, the frame and forks looked similar, although wheel-spindle offset was reduced. Full-width hubs were fitted, together with an older version of the four-speed gearbox, but the model lacked the lightweight parts used on the works machines. It was good, but by 1960 the move to smaller machines and two-strokes had already begun.

The remaining four models in the range were twins, two of 496 cc and two of 693 cc. The smaller machines were the Meteor Minor and Meteor Minor Sports, while the larger models were the Super Meteor and Constellation. All had four-speed gearboxes and many of the design features that were common to the Bullet engine.

The twins differed from the singles in having chain-driven camshafts high in the crankcase and to the front and rear of the cylinders. Similar to the singles were the oil pumps and oil compartment in the rear of the crankcase, to which the gearbox

was bolted. Inside was a one-piece iron crankshaft with split big-end shell bearings. The heads and barrels were separate, the former in light alloy with integral rocker boxes, and the latter in iron. A single Amal carburettor supplied the mixture.

The camshafts had their cams at each end, so the pushrods ran through tunnels in the outer corners of the barrels. Ignition was by coil, the points being housed behind the engine where their cam was chain driven. An alternator was mounted on the left in the primary chaincase, where a duplex chain drove the clutch and gearbox.

Cycle parts were the same as for the Crusader and Bullet models, with open frame, telescopics, pivoted rear fork, casquette, dualseat and all-purpose centre section. The wheels also had the same 17 in. diameter, but both front and rear brakes were 7 in. in full-width hubs. An Airflow fairing was available for all these models.

The Sports version, which was new for 1960, was very similar to the standard machine, but it had different cams to lift the power a trifle. It also had chrome-plated mudguards and other cosmetic changes.

Above **Royal Enfield Continental of 1963, with 248 cc and lovely 'jelly mould' tank**

Above left **The 1963 Bullet retained its 346 cc, but in a Crusader engine form**

The Super Meteor was an enlarged version of the original 500 Twin, which preceded the Meteor Minor, and it was based on this plus the top half of the 346 cc Bullet. Construction was similar to the 496 cc twin, including the cycle parts. As with the smaller model it had siamezed pipes, but the fuel tank was bigger and it had the dual 6 in. front brake together with the 7 in. rear.

Known to its owners as the 'Connie', the Constellation was the sports version of the big twin, with a more powerful engine, magneto ignition and, for 1960, twin Monoblocs. The finish was brighter than that of the Super Meteor, and both could be fitted with the Airflow fairing, in which case twin exhaust systems were installed.

That completed the range, all of which were carried forward for 1961, most with little alteration. The most obvious change occurred on the 693 cc

twins, which were given a degree of rear enclosure that linked the rear mudguard and seat to the toolbox lids. The 346 cc trials model became available to special order only. The entire range continued for 1962, but with more changes and two new models.

Effectively unchanged were the Prince, Crusader, Clipper II, Bullets, Clipper, Trials model, Meteor Minor, Super Meteor and Constellation. Of the remaining pair, the Crusader Sports was fitted with a styled rear mudguard, which also formed a surround to the seat base. Later in the year, the option of a five-speed gearbox became available for this model. The other machine, the Meteor Minor Sports, was changed in respect of the front brake, which was altered to the dual 6 in. type.

Both new models were of 248 cc and based on the Crusader engine unit. One was the Super 5, which was in essence the Sports Crusader with a five-speed gearbox and leading-link front forks. It had the styled rear mudguard and a 7 in. front brake.

The second model was very different and was listed as the 250 Trials. It was derived from the

Above **Royal Enfield Super 5 for 1963, with five speeds and leading-link forks, but with that Oriental make close by**

Above left **The 500 Sports Twin in 1963, its only year of production**

Left **Factory scrambler based on the 250 Crusader from around 1963, but it was never a production model**

Sports Crusader and retained that model's coil ignition, so it came with an alternator and battery. The exhaust was tucked in at waist level on the right with a small silencer, and a wide-ratio gearbox was fitted.

The frame was standard, but the forks were special with two-way damping. The wheel sizes were 21 in. front and 18 in. rear with suitable tyres, and alloy mudguards were fitted, the front one following the tyre closely. Unfortunately, the result was too heavy, and the engine had an irritating habit of cutting out for no reason at awkward moments. With the move to two-stroke trials machines well under way, it was hardly surprising that few of the 250 Trials model were sold.

The range was pruned drastically for 1963, the discontinued models being the Prince, Crusader, both Bullets, Clipper, 350 Works Replica Trials, Meteor Minor, Super Meteor and the Constellation in solo form. However, there were some replacements, which left a total of nine models in the range. Five were based on the 248 cc unit engine, while another had the same stretched to 346 cc.

Among the existing singles, the Clipper II took over the Crusader role, and the Sports version

regained its standard rear mudguard, but kept its five-speed option. The Super 5 was given an unsprung front mudguard, which looked much better with the leading-link forks. The 250 Trials was offered to special order only, but there were few takers.

The fifth, and new, 248 cc model was the Continental, which was a sports machine with some special styling features of its own. The basis of the Continental was the Super 5 engine unit in the standard frame, but it was fitted with telescopic front forks. Wheels were 17 in., and a 7 in. front brake was fitted. However, it was the fixtures and fittings that set the model off.

First and foremost was the petrol tank, which was formed in the Italian style and referred to as the 'jelly mould' type. Added to this was a snap-action filler cap in the best racer style, and at the top of the forks the casquette had been replaced by an instrument panel. This carried a speedo-meter and rev-counter placed side by side, and it lay behind a small flyscreen, which carried the front number plate across its base.

Thruxton drop bars and ball-end control levers completed the racer image, which was set off by a chrome-plated front mudguard with a single rear stay. The guard was matched by another at the back where the suspension unit springs were

Left **The Crusader Sports, which had low bars and its footrests set further back than the standard model, pictured outside Kew Gardens**

Below **John Hartle and Geoff Duke at Oulton Park, early in 1964, with the Royal Enfield GP5 prototype**

partly exposed. To complete the picture, the front brake had an airscoop on the backplate.

The 346 cc model in the Crusader style was the New Bullet, which looked much the same, except for a couple of extra fins on the barrel. Internally, there were a built-up crankshaft and other changes.

The remaining machines were twins, and the sole 496 cc model was the 500 Sports Twin, which was the Meteor Minor Sports with a 7 in. front brake. The 693 cc Constellation was available only as a sidecar machine, and to this end was detuned to the Meteor specification, with low compression ratio, one carburettor and coil ignition. A siamezed exhaust system was fitted as standard, twin systems being an option. To suit sidecar use, the machine had lowered gearing, reduced fork trail, stiff suspension and a steering damper.

New to the range was the 736 cc Interceptor, which was similar to the Constellation but had the enlarged engine. There were detail changes too, among them parallel inlet stubs for the twin carburettors, a rev-counter drive and the choice of three camshafts. Ignition was by magneto, and the cycle side was the same as the Connie. As with the other models, an Airflow fairing was available, but not the lighter and slimmer Sportsflow. This was introduced for 1963 and listed for the singles only.

There were more changes to the range for 1964, the Super 5, 250 Trials, 500 Sports Twin and sidecar Constellation being dropped. The range was padded out again by listing the Crusader Sports, Continental and Interceptor in standard and de luxe forms. The former had painted finishes instead of plating, and the Continental version came without the rev-counter and flyscreen. The de luxe Interceptor had a 12-volt electrical system as well as its chrome plate, but otherwise both versions were very similar and had the same list of options.

The list of options was extended to the Clipper II in an attempt to unload unwanted five-speed gearboxes and leading-link forks. Otherwise,

however, this model continued unchanged, as did the New Bullet, but the remaining pair of machines were new two-strokes. These were the Turbo Twin and the Turbo Twin Sports, both of which had the 249 cc Villiers 4T engine in a set of Crusader cycle parts. They had a four-speed gearbox, 6 in. brakes in full-width hubs and 17 in. wheels. These machines differed from the other models in having a separate headlamp shell, and the Sports version also had dropped bars and chrome-plated mudguards and tank panels.

Late in 1963 another two-stroke had been seen in prototype form. This was a scrambles model powered by a 247 cc Villiers Starmaker engine.

Below left **Royal Enfield scrambler with Villiers Starmaker engine for 1965**

Below **The Turbo Twin Sports two-stroke for 1965, with Villiers 4T engine in Crusader cycle parts**

Early in 1964 it was joined by a second machine, which was built for road racing, and both would be in the range for 1965. The racing model was promoted by a works team managed by Geoff Duke, with John Hartle as the rider.

The scrambler had the normal Villiers engine with four-speed gearbox in a frame based on the standard version with a duplex cradle added to support the engine unit. Suspension was by leading links at the front and pivoted fork at the rear, where the suspension units were laid down a little. The remaining fittings were appropriate to the scrambles task and included braced bars, a 21 in. front wheel, suitable tyres and a short seat.

The road racer was called the GP5, and although a Starmaker engine was used at first, it was soon replaced by a Royal Enfield power unit. This was based on an Alpha bottom half, which dictated the engine dimensions and the 246 cc capacity. The top half was Enfield and followed normal two-stroke practice for the period, having an air-cooled alloy barrel with iron liner.

A five-speed Albion gearbox was bolted to the back of the crankcase, with a heat-dissipating casting between the two. The engine/gearbox assembly was installed in a duplex frame with a single top tube, while the suspension was the same as the scrambler's. Suitable racing equipment was added, and a one-piece fibreglass tank, seat and tail unit fitted. The tank held some 7 gallons of fuel. A fairing was supplied with the model, which proved to be fast on the circuits, but was not too reliable.

Meanwhile, the road range showed few changes for 1965, but the standard Crusader Sports, Continental and Interceptor were dropped. The Clipper II and Crusader Sports had a modified silencer, as did the Continental, which also received fork gaiters. However, there were no changes to the Turbo Twins or the New Bullet. The Interceptor was only built in its long-wheelbase, American form, and there were two new models, both further varieties of the Crusader.

One of the new machines was the Olympic, which seemed to be an attempt to use up parts no-one really wanted, as it had the leading-link forks, and the Super 5 casquette and styled rear mudguard. The remainder comprised the normal Crusader engine and four-speed gearbox in the standard frame with dropped bars and a special colour scheme.

The other machine was different and much more up-to-date, as it was in pure café-racer style, matching the image that the young customers of the period required. With the learner limit still at 250 cc, it fitted in very well. The model was given the name Continental GT, being based on the existing model but with a tuned engine and a lot more style.

The GT came about because the firm had asked its dealers what they wanted, then built a prototype, and finally given their own apprentices a free rein to add their own ideas. The result was the noisy, uncomfortable, stripped-down, race-style machine that the young craved for.

The Continental GT had the Crusader engine with a raised compression ratio of 9.5:1 and the five-speed gearbox. There was a long bellmouth for the Monobloc, with no nonsense about air filters, and the exhaust was a cranked and swept-back pipe. A massive plastic breather pipe swept up from the crankcase to run to the rear mudguard.

Instruments were the same as on the Continental, but there were also clip-on bars, rearsets, folding footrests and a humped seat. The screen and ball-ended levers came from the Continental. Gaiters were fitted to the front forks, and the front hub carried large alloy cooling discs—a common feature on racers of the period. The rear springs were fully exposed. There was no toolbox, but the youth of the time carried their tools in a jacket pocket.

The machine was set off by a large fibreglass fuel tank, which had knee recesses and a quick-action filler cap. It was finished in red with the marque on

Left **Royal Enfield Interceptor of 1969, with wet-sump engine, and Norton forks and front hub—a rugged performer**

Right **A batch of 1968 Interceptors, which retained the traditional dry-sump crankcase favoured by Enfields**

each side in white letters. The frame was silver and the blade mudguards red to match the tank.

An outrageous café racer might have been what youth wanted, but by then the Japanese were offering some comprehensively equipped machines, and often parental influence would steer a youngster to them. In a contracting market, this placed the Enfield firm in financial difficulties, and for 1966 the range had to be reduced.

Out went the Clipper II, Olympic, Continental, Turbo Twin, 247 cc Scrambler and New Bullet, while the few Interceptors that were built went for export. Four 250s were left, one of which was the GP5. This was only ever made in very small numbers, and its production ceased early in the year. That left the Crusader Sports and Turbo Twin Sports, neither of which was altered, but both were dropped later that year. The one other model was the Continental GT, which gained a fibreglass cover for its electrics, but it lasted only a little longer, being discontinued early in 1967 when the company was taken over by Norton Villiers.

The takeover might have been the end of the Enfield machine, but during a succession of takeovers and business deals, the Interceptor continued to be built in small numbers, and late in 1967 it reappeared on the home market. Changes were made, but the machine was much as before. It was given coil ignition, Concentrics, twin exhausts, a small fuel tank and cooling discs on the front hub.

Late in 1968, the Interceptor was superseded by the Series II model, which differed considerably, only the frame and rear hub remaining as they were. The engine was based on the traditional Enfield twin, but a major change was to wet-sump lubrication, which meant new crankcase castings. Thus, there was only one oil pump, and the timing side was revised to reflect both this and the move of the ignition points to the end of the exhaust camshaft.

Twin Concentrics and twin exhaust systems looked after the gases, and a duplex primary chain drove a four-speed Albion gearbox. The frame was fitted with gaitered Norton forks, which held an 8 in. Norton front brake. Either a 2- or 4-gallon tank could be specified, and there was a new seat. There were options of an air cleaner, oil cooler, skid plate and seat rail, all of which were fitted as standard for 1970.

During that year Enfield finally had to stop production, but even that did not bring the story to an end. The engines went on to be used in the Rickman chassis early in 1970. This machine displayed the usual immaculate finish and was fitted with disc brakes on both wheels—then very rare. Later, the machine became the Rickman Enfield and, as such, one of the last of the big vertical twins in a world of refined and sophisticated Japanese fours. The oddest feature was the footrests, which were mounted on the exhaust pipes, but most owners of the 130 or so built liked them.

Sapphire

The Sapphire marque was founded by Roger Kyffin, who was a successful scrambler in the 1950s, riding a TR5 Triumph. When this model went out of production, he replaced it with a special based on a Triumph 5TA unit engine squeezed into a Dot frame. The result was fast, light and a winner, so the orders rolled in and Roger set to work.

The production Sapphire retained the Dot leading-link forks, but not much else. The frame underwent major surgery, including the addition of a new subframe, emerging as a neat and functional duplex assembly. The small matter of obtaining the engine and gearbox units was solved by visiting Triumph dealers all over the country and buying sets of parts as spares. These were assembled into complete units, and some 75 were put together before Meriden caught on to what was happening and stopped it.

These machines were built during the 1963–66 period, and after the first two dozen or so, Roger switched to his own frame, which carried the oil in its tubes and was fitted with Ceriani front forks.

After the Triumph, he tried using a BSA unit twin, but Small Heath also refused to supply him with engines, so he turned to Villiers and built smaller machines. He produced the Red Rose trials and Moto-Cross scrambler models, both in kit form and powered by 246 cc engines. The former had the 37A and the latter the 36A.

When Villiers stopped building engines, Roger had to cease manufacture, but he remained in the trade as a dealer.

The Sapphire with Triumph engine and Dot forks, a very nice machine built by Roger Kyffin. Note early spelling of the machine's name

Saracen

Scorpion

These machines were built by Robin Goodfellow, who founded the firm in 1967 in Cirencester and used the Sachs 125 cc engine with five-speed gearbox for his project. This went into a very well-made frame fitted with REH or Metal Profiles telescopic front forks, while both wheels had Rickman conical hubs.

The machines were sold in kit form and, although expensive, found plenty of customers during the 1967–71 period. Unfortunately, the high price was not actually high enough, so the company was losing money. Because of this, it was sold to David Brand in 1972. He reorganized production and introduced machines with larger engines. These proved less successful than the original 125 cc unit, and without Goodfellow the marque was no longer able to compete with its Spanish rivals and ceased production in the 1970s.

The Scorpion make appeared briefly on the British motorcycle scene and is remembered for its unusual T-frame, which was constructed from sheet steel, being light, rigid and strong. The machine was announced early in 1963 as a trials model and was available assembled or in kit form. Normally, it was powered by a Villiers 9E or 32A unit, but it could also be fitted with a BSA B40.

The frame was constructed by welding together box sections, one acting as the top beam and one the seat tube, with a pair running back to the tops of the rear suspension units. Bolted to this basic structure was a frame loop formed from square-section tube. By changing the latter, it was a simple matter to accommodate alternative engines.

The pivoted rear fork legs were also formed from square-section tubing, but at the front there were Armstrong leading-link forks. Both wheels had full-width hubs with 6 in. brakes, and the mudguards were fibreglass, the rear version being formed in one piece with the seat base and the rear number-plate mount. Fuel tanks of 1- and 2-gallon capacity were available, also formed in fibreglass.

The fixtures and fittings were much the same as those used on most other trials models, but thanks to the frame design the Scorpion was a good deal lighter than the rest at a claimed 200 lb (including the standard engine with its iron barrel).

The trials model was soon followed by a scrambles version, listed as the Moto-cross Mk4 and powered by a 246 cc engine. This could be a stock Villiers 36A or one with a Marcelle or Parkinson conversion. There was a further option in the form of a 247 cc Starmaker unit. To suit engines which had the exhaust port set on their centre line, there was a twin-tube frame loop which straddled it. In most other respects, the machine was the same as the trials model without the road equipment.

By late 1963 the production design was rolling,

Above **1964 Scorpion with Villiers Starmaker twin-carburettor engine fitted to its unusual, sheet-steel, box-section frame**

Left **The Scorpion kit, as supplied, shown here with 36A engine plus top-half conversion, and also full-circle crankshaft and cases**

Below **The road-racing Scorpion prototype, on show with spine frame and their own design of engine**

and the two basic models were listed in various guises. The trials model with standard 32A engine became the Type 2, while the Replica was the same but fitted with a Parkinson conversion. The scrambler came in the same two forms, as the Moto-cross Mk4 and the Replica, but there was also a third machine. This was the Moto-cross Type 4 Special, which had the Starmaker engine and a different finish.

All models were available assembled or in kit form, either with or without the engine and gearbox unit. Options took the form of the Parkinson conversion, Alpha crankshaft, alloy tank and a detachable centre stand.

Late in 1964 a new range was announced, comprising two scramblers and a road racer. The last caught the eye and was one of a number of 250s that appeared in the mid-1960s for the clubman racer. The engine was Scorpion's own design and had an Alpha crankshaft, but the rest of the parts were of their own design and manufacture. It followed conventional lines for the time, with air cooling, GP2 Amal and expansion exhaust, while the gearbox was a five-speed Albion.

The engine was hung from a tubular spine frame based on a massive tube that was bent to form the top and seat tubes and which had a welded-on light subframe. Suspension was by telescopic front forks and Girling-controlled, pivoted rear fork, and both wheels had big Oldani brakes. Standard equipment included a rev-counter, clip-ons, racing seat and rear-mounted footrests.

The Avenger MX4 scrambler had the same engine with modifications to lower the power band a bit. It had the forks from the road racer, but it retained 6 in. brakes and a four-speed gearbox. The other scrambler was the Scrambles Special, which was simply the Mk4 with the Starmaker engine under a new name. The other Scorpion machines were no longer listed.

Soon, however, the supply of Villiers engines began to dry up, and the Scorpion engine never progressed beyond the show prototype, which had carried the label Racer 250 GP5. As quickly as the Scorpion name had appeared, it vanished from the lists as if it had never existed.

Scott

The Scott was a truly special motorcycle from first to last, and one that evoked strong reactions from owners, riders and motorcyclists in general. In design terms, it was an anachronism for, with few exceptions, the machines had a twin-cylinder two-stroke engine with central flywheel, overhung cranks and inaccessible primary drive. It took this form in 1908 and was the same half a century later.

During those years the company had experienced more ups and downs than most. They won the Senior TT in 1912 and 1913, but two years later Alfred Scott had moved on, and those left behind stuck to his one basic design. They kept going until 1950 when they went into voluntary liquidation. The old works at Saltaire was disposed of and the name sold to Matt Holder. His company, Aerco Jig and Tool, was based in Birmingham, but it was some years before production could continue.

Eventually, the Scott returned to the market in small numbers, still based on the same format as before. It was listed with a choice of 497 or 598 cc engines, which were parallel twins with water cooling and inclined block, sharing a common stroke. The crankcase form and primary drive were the same as earlier models, as were the head, block and general arrangements.

By 1958 an alternator had been added on the left, being attached to the crankcase door. Its rotor was turned by the end of the big-end journal, the same arrangement on the right driving a combined oil pump and distributor built into the door on that side.

The central primary chain drove a three-speed gearbox, which had a pre-war type of positive-stop mechanism. The frame was more up-to-date, however, with duplex tubes and pivoted rear fork. There were Scott telescopic forks at the front, a dualseat and the familiar wedge tank with the radiator in front of it. The front hub had a 7 in. brake in each side, and the 8 in. rear drum was in a full-width hub to match.

Above **Matt Holder and the 345 cc racing Scott, around 1964. Few were built, and then came Yamaha**

Right **Scott engine, showing the crankcase door which carried the distributor and double oil pump, plus other long-standing details**

In this form, the Scott continued to be offered in the 598 cc size as standard, but with the 497 cc engine to special order for year after year. Production was always in very small numbers, but continue it did, through the 1960s and 1970s and on into the 1980s, when it was available to special order.

Matt Holder kept the name going right up to his death, and his life-long enthusiasm for the marque led to other machines being investigated and prototypes built. One such appeared in the news in 1964, being a 345 cc road racer. Its engine retained the inclined cylinders, but in this application they were air cooled and separate. The two crankshafts were conventional, each having two full-circle wheels which were keyed and bolted through the central flywheel—a feature from the past that had been retained.

The crankcase was one casting with doors on the sides and back and an open centre section for

the flywheel. The points were on the right-hand end of the crankshaft, and the primary drive on the left, while the five-speed Albion gearbox was mounted separately in a set of plates. The engine design allowed the box to be bolted to the back of the crankcase for production road models. It also permitted the construction of a water-cooled 498 cc unit.

The machine was conventional in design, other than in having leading-link forks. It had an 8 in. twin-leading-shoe brake at the front, and a 7 in. version at the rear, with 18 in. rims for both wheels. The model continued to be listed together with the road twins until 1967, but few, if any, were built.

Thus, the Scott remained one of the rarest machines of the 1960s and, as always, an enigma to most motorcyclists. In 1971 the engine formed the basis of the Silk machine, which was intended to continue the original Scott concept of a good engine in a light frame. From this comes performance and good handling, but in limited production the result is expensive. For all that, the Silk was built in small numbers for most of the 1970s.

The Scott twin of 1960. Little changed for many years, but the suspension, seat and lines were amended to suit the times

Sprite

The Sprite firm came about in the same manner as many others in the motorcycle field. It was formed by Frank Hipkin and his partner, Fred Evans, because Frank had built his own machines for trials and scrambles use and had enjoyed a good deal of success with them. This encouraged other riders to ask him to build replicas for them, and before long he was in business.

The first Sprite was based on a modified Cotton frame with Norton front forks and a fibreglass rear mudguard assembly. The power unit was a combination of an Alpha bottom half and a modified Greeves barrel, being coupled to an Albion gearbox. The machine had a very functional appearance.

By March 1964 the development model had been built, and the first five production machines were in hand. The engine remained much the same, but the frame was now truly a Sprite, with duplex down-tubes, pivoted-fork rear suspension and all-welded construction. The front forks had become the gaitered AMC heavyweight type, and full-width hubs were used in both wheels.

An Amal Monobloc supplied the mixture, and the exhaust ran high on the left. The rear mudguard continued to be in fibreglass, as did the side panels which enclosed the air filter, battery and ignition coil. The seat base was also fibreglass. A slim tank completed a very purposeful machine, which was sold in kit form to avoid purchase tax.

By July it was in full production, but with a Miller magneto, duplex primary chain and closer gearbox ratios. Also on the stocks by then were a trials model and a scrambles frame kit designed for a 500 cc unit-construction Triumph engine.

The trials frame remained duplex, but it was narrower than the scrambles version, and the rear mudguard was extended to form a number-plate

Sprite scrambles frame kit, assembled and fitted with a unit Triumph engine

mount. The engine was a 246 cc A-series Villiers, either in standard form or with a Greeves alloy barrel.

The scrambles frame kit was sold complete less engine, the frame itself differing from the others in that its top member was of rectangular section and acted as the oil tank together with the duplex cradle. In other respects, it followed the lines of the two-stroke frame, the cycle parts being the same.

From the beginning of 1965 the front suspension was changed to leading-link forks, and the head bearings were amended to taper rollers. The headstock dimensions were such that owners could opt for AMC, BSA or Ceriani forks if they wished without having to do any more than fit them. The leading-links had a fork loop that ran round the back of the wheel, the pivot being midway along this. Two Girling suspension units controlled wheel movement, and the brake backplate was anchored to the fork leg with a link.

In March 1965 the firm announced another innovation in that customers could collect their kits directly from the works at Oldbury in Worcestershire, which reduced the price further. At the same time, they could try out complete models on a piece of adjoining land. Both moves proved popular with the public.

Coupled with this news was the announcement

that the trials frame had been revised to reduce its weight, and that a second scrambles frame kit was available for engines with a separate gearbox.

There were two new models for 1966, both powered by the 247 cc Villiers Starmaker engine, and both given the name Monza. The trials machine had plenty of ground clearance and a frame assembled from two loops mounted close together. This was similar to, but lighter than the existing frame, and the subframe was short with the rear suspension units angled a little. They were connected to the rear fork ahead of the wheel spindle.

The front forks remained leading-link, but with longer Girlings to give a softer action and more wheel movement. The seat was minimal with a fibreglass base, the mudguards being in the same material. The fuel tank was small and slim, and the rest of the equipment was pure trials, right down to the small speedometer head mounted low on the frame by the engine.

The Monza scrambler had the cycle parts from the standard model with the Starmaker exhaust system tucked under the power unit and between the frame rails. The seat was well padded, unlike the trials version, and there were side panels. Between them was an inner mudguard moulding, which incorporated a still-air chamber to contain

Above **Sprite scrambler of 1969, fitted with a 125 cc Zundapp engine and carrying the American Eagle tank badge**

Above *left* **1968 Sprite with their own 360 cc engine, which was a close copy of the Husqvarna unit**

the air filter and supply the carburettor.

This line of models continued for 1967, and the same year saw the frame kits modified to accept Maico or Husqvarna engines. This proved to be a good move, for Villiers stopped engine production around 1968 and supplies dried up. Consequently, Sprite were able to continue offering kits, and then announced their own 360 cc engine. This turned out to be a near copy of the Husqvarna unit, but it kept the firm going.

For 1969 the engine was enlarged to 399 cc, according to the bore and stroke dimensions, but 405 cc was claimed in the literature of the time. It had an alloy top half with pressed-in cylinder liner and was well finned, the head fins being angled to direct cooling air to the plug. An Amal supplied the petroil mixture, and a Bosch flywheel magneto ignited it. The four-speed gearbox was of the cross-over design, having the gear primary drive on the left and the output sprocket on the right.

The cycle parts continued in the Sprite tradition with a duplex cradle frame, but telescopic front forks were now standard, and both wheels had conical hubs with 6 in. brakes. Normal scrambles equipment was included, and the exhaust system continued to live under the engine and between the frame tubes.

The big two-stroke was joined by a 245 cc version late in 1969. This had much in common with the larger model in both engine and chassis. Before this model appeared, a new trials machine was introduced, which set a trend by having a 125 cc Sachs engine and reduced dimensions to create a mini-bike. This had all the features of a full-size machine, but it was lighter and easier to handle. It could be supplied with or without lights. As always, all the models came in kit form.

In this way, Sprite carried on into the 1970s with plenty of innovation, but sadly a major deal with an American firm went wrong. They placed a major order, took delivery and went bankrupt, which stopped the company. However, it recovered later to continue with other products.

Sun

Sun motorcycles existed before World War 1, but production lapsed in the 1930s, being revived again in post-war years. By 1960 it had come to a halt once more, but the firm continued in the market with a pair of scooters.

The first of the scooters dated from 1957 and was the 98 cc Geni. By 1960 it had been modified a little, becoming the MkII with a Villiers 6F engine and two-speed gearbox. This drove the rear wheel by open chain. Both wheels were spoked and of 15 in. diameter—unusual features for a scooter. Suspension was by short leading links at the front, with a pivoted fork at the rear.

The Geni bodywork followed normal scooter lines, having a rear enclosure, which supported the dualseat, and a front apron, but between the two there was a distinct tunnel. This shrouded the engine unit, which was mounted well forward. The engine's position coupled with the large wheels played an important part in giving the machine good handling. Two panels gave access to the sparking plug and carburettor. The accessory list included a wire shopping basket to fit behind the apron, windscreen, holdall and rear carrier.

The second scooter was the Sunwasp, which was introduced during 1959 and had the 174 cc Villiers 2L engine with three-speed gearbox, fan cooling and Siba electric starter. The frame was based on the usual large main tube with attachment brackets, and the suspension comprised leading links at the front and a pivoted fork at the rear. The wheels were of pressed steel and 10 in. diameter with 6 in. brakes.

The fuel tank was at the rear of the cylinder over the gearbox, and the batteries were mounted to the rear and to each side of the engine. The dualseat was hinged along one side, and a well-valanced rear mudguard fitted under the panelling. The body was of typical scooter design and very similar to the Dayton Flamenco and Panther Princess, although there were detail variations. It had a flat floor between the apron and rear section, and there were twin lockers in the back of the apron with a fascia above.

No less than three pedals rose through the floor, the left-hand one dealing with the rear brake. The other two, which were on the right, were linked to the gear-change mechanism—the rider pressed the right-hand one to change up, and the one on the left to change down.

Engine access was through side panels, while the rear body could be removed completely after releasing five bolts. Neat details were the gauze vents in the dualseat sides and the asbestos seat-pan lining, which protected the seat from engine heat.

At the end of the year, the Geni was dropped and the Sunwasp was replaced by a new version in two forms for 1961. These were the Sunwasp MkII de luxe and the Sunwasp KS, both with the 174 cc Villiers 2L engine, fan cooling and three speeds. The MkII retained the electric starter, while the KS had 6-volt electrics and a kickstart pedal. Both had the option of a four-speed gearbox.

The changes were mainly to suit production methods, but included a one-piece apron, larger lockers and a lock for the right-hand locker door. A lifting handle was added to the rear of the body, and there were other detail improvements. However, the days were numbered for Sun, and these stylish scooters were withdrawn from the market at the end of 1961.

The Sun Geni scooter prototype in 1957, prior to painting and fitting of the rear chain

Sunbeam

When the BSA and Triumph group finally joined the post-war scooter boom, they offered two model sizes under each make, the BSA version being sold under the Sunbeam label. Earlier, this had been the name on the tanks of some very well finished pre-war models, and then a pair of post-war in-line twins until 1958. Older owners were none too pleased, therefore, to see the name reappearing on a scooter.

The machine was offered with either a 172 cc two-stroke engine or a 249 cc, twin-cylinder four-stroke with overhead valves. The latter was listed with electric or kick starting, and both were launched late in 1958 after a very long gestation period. The twin reached the market soon after, but the single was delayed until late in 1959.

Although the two engines were totally different, the transmission, general layout and nearly all the chassis were common to both versions. Differences amounted to silencer position, exhaust pipes, electrics and engine mounting brackets.

The single-cylinder engine was based on the BSA D7 Bantam, but there were few common parts. One of the few was the alloy cylinder head, but the barrel differed in its exhaust port, and the flywheels were smaller. The piston, rod and big-end came from the D7, but the crankshafts were extended. A Wico-Pacy generator was fitted to the right-hand one, and the clutch to the left, so the latter component ran at engine speed.

The generator had a cooling fan attached to its rotor, both fan and the engine top half being

Sunwasp scooter on test late in 1959, with Bob Currie doing the riding of this 174 cc, electric-start model

cowled to assist cooling. Initially, the carburettor was mounted on a stub, but later this was changed to an elbow to improve access. The exhaust pipe ran down to a silencer under the engine, with a tailpipe on the right.

The two cylinders of the four-stroke engine were set across the frame, with the gear-driven camshaft to the rear of the crankcase. The valves ran in a row across the head, but while the inner inlets were vertical, the exhausts lay outwards at an angle. Thus, their rockers had fore-and-aft spindles, while the inlet rocker spindles were parallel to the camshaft.

The engine was all alloy, with one casting for the head and another for the block, crankcase and gearbox shell. The crankshaft was a one-piece forging, and a generator with cooling fan was mounted on the right-hand end. In this instance, the rotor also carried a starter ring gear, which meshed with a Lucas pre-engaged starter motor when required. The clutch was on the left-hand end of the crankshaft, and the points were on the same end of the camshaft. The right-hand end of this operated a single-plunger oil pump from an eccentric to supply the wet-sump lubrication

system. A single Zenith carburettor was tucked in behind the engine, and an exhaust pipe ran back from each side of the head to a small silencer positioned right in the tail of the machine.

Apart from the engine, both single and twin were essentially the same as regards transmission and rear-wheel drive. The clutch was on the left with its operating lever outside the cover, and the primary drive was taken from a point between the engine and clutch. This drive was by gears, and here there was variation, as the single had a greater reduction ratio than the twin.

The gearbox was based on the version fitted to the BSA C15 and Triumph Cub models, having four speeds and positive-stop gear selection. This was linked by rod to a single pedal, which was pushed forwards or backwards to change gear. A second pedal at the rear of the footboard selected neutral from the second-gear position.

A kickstart pedal on the right was linked by a short chain to the gearbox and hence to the engine. The final pedal, on the left of the footboard, was for the rear brake.

The final drive to the rear wheel was by duplex chain, which was fully enclosed by alloy castings.

These also acted as the rear suspension pivoted arm and were arranged to swing about the centre of the gearbox output sprocket. Thus, a simple blade tensioner could be used to keep the chain running smoothly. Additional castings and a support member kept the mechanics enclosed.

The complete engine and gearbox assembly was installed in a tubular scooter frame, which was unusual in that it had duplex front tubes rather than a single large tube. It also differed in having the headstock tube bolted to the main frame so that it sat at the junction of the two frame tubes.

The front suspension was telescopic, but with a single leg only, on the left. This incorporated two tubes; one for the spring and the other for the hydraulic damper. A single spring-and-damper unit on the left dealt with the rear suspension. The interchangeable wheels were pressed steel of 10 in. diameter and were mounted on stub axles. Both brakes were 5 in. and cable operated.

The bodywork was built up from steel pressings and had a fixed front mudguard, but access was limited by small panels. The fuel tank was under the seat, which was hinged, and the one or two batteries were in boxes on the back of the apron.

The second battery was only fitted to the electric-start model.

All models were finished in a polychromatic green and carried Sunbeam badges to distinguish them from their Triumph equivalents. They were listed as the B1, B2 and B2S, the first being the two-stroke and the last the electric-start twin. A good array of accessories was listed to go with them in the usual scooter fashion.

The trio of models continued in this form for 1960, but for 1961 they became available in red or blue, or in two-tone with a cream apron. For 1962 the exhaust system of the twin was amended so that the right-hand pipe ran across in front of the engine to join the left. From here a single pipe ran to the silencer.

Otherwise, the machines continued as they were until mid-1964 when the twins were dropped, followed by the single a year later. The firm had really been too late in the market to achieve high sales, and it was better for BSA to follow other market trends, which they did.

Left **Factory line-up of BSA Sunbeam and Triumph Tigress scooters at Small Heath in 1959. Badges and colour determined marque**

Right **Sammy Miller, flanked by two Sunbeam girls, on the BSA stand at an Earls Court show**

Triton

Triton is the title of the cult café racer of the 1960s, a machine that was the epitome of all that was going on at the time. It fulfilled the desire for a motorcycle that was fast, handled well and, above all, differed from the mainstream. All manner of specials were built with this end in view, but the centre of fashion was the combination of a Triumph engine and Norton featherbed frame.

One of the early factors that brought this about was 500 cc car racing. This began as a cheap racing class soon after World War 2, and in its early years most drivers used a JAP engine. Soon, some turned to the twin-cam Manx Norton unit, and before long this became essential. However, Norton refused to sell engines alone, so racers began to buy complete Manx Nortons, removing just the engine and gearbox from them. This produced a supply of complete chassis, into which most single- and twin-cylinder engines could be slotted.

Early Tritons were usually built for racing, the Triumph engine being a natural choice for the power unit. It was available in 500 and 650 cc form, and enough had been tuned and raced over the years for the necessary techniques to be known and parts to be available. It was also a good deal cheaper than a Manx, and the job of building one was well within many riders' capabilities.

So Tritons began to be raced, and soon this style of machine was copied for road use. The first ones were usually built with Manx cycle parts, but before long those from the 88 were pressed into service. These had the advantage of having full road equipment, even if the brakes were not the conical-hub type.

Standards of build varied a good deal, as did the

list of parts used, for not all Tritons began with a complete Norton chassis. Often, only a frame was available, so other forks and wheels began to appear, together with all manner of detail fittings. Both wideline and slimline frames were used, as were unit and pre-unit engines. Capacity was inevitably 500 or 650 cc at first, the latter becoming more usual for road work. Few riders opted for the 500 unit engine, which looked wrong in the featherbed frame, but many sought more power from the 650.

Triton with Metalflake paint finish for the tank, and fitted with most of the usual goodies

Extra power could come from tuning, a big-bore kit or, in later years, by using the T140 engine. As time passed, more special parts came to be used, and the options increased. The same applied to the chassis, modified forks, bigger and better brakes, special box-section rear forks, alternative hubs and all manner of customized items being used.

This was a natural development, and it had to be expected as an automatic follow-on to the basic reason for the machine's existance. It began as a means of self expression, but as soon as there were two of them, they had to progress to retain their individuality. Most owners succeeded in this aim, but often the machines lost some of the charm of the original in the process. Hot camshafts and lumpy pistons made for an intractable motor for road use, while extra cosmetics meant extra weight.

For many, the original was best. In this form, the Triton had a pre-unit 650 engine with Triumph gearbox and primary drive. The frame was the all-

Above **1970 Dresda Triton with the Trident engine, rather than the usual twin**

Above left **Eric Cheney scrambles machine of 1959, with Norton frame and forks. Triumph engine and wheels, plus a BSA gearbox**

Left **Dave Degens built this neat Dresda Triton for Philip Hicks in 1965—the tank was bright red**

welded wideline type, and the forks the short Roadholders. These had no top shrouds, as they held clip-on bars and headlamp stays, but there were rubber gaiters to protect the stanchions.

Both wheels had Norton full-width hubs, with the optional twin-leading-shoe brake at the front. Mudguards were narrow blades with a chrome-plated finish, while the headlamp and a good few other parts were given the same treatment.

The petrol tank, which was often held in place by a strap, could be in alloy or fibreglass, and the central oil tank was to match. The former always had a quick-action filler cap, which was as important a feature as the swept-back exhaust pipes and matching speedometer and rev-counter on the fork crown. The Norton friction steering damper would be retained together with its wing-nut adjuster. The dualseat was styled like that on a Manx Norton.

From this base, owners progressed in every direction. The concept became so popular that engine plates became available commercially, as did many other parts, and this process was taken to its natural conclusion with the production of complete machines.

One of the first to sell completed Tritons was Dave Degens, who founded Dresda Autos in 1959 to market them. His machines ranked with the best and were always well made and finished. In the mid-1960s he had an arrangement with the Rickmans, the result being the Dresda Metisse (see page 148).

In time, Degens began building his own frames and later used Japanese engines with equal success because he never lost the habit of doing the job properly. With the revival of interest in classic machines during the 1980s, he found customers in Japan who wanted Tritons, so the wheel turned full circle and he began to build them again.

True to the Triton theme, they continued to be individual, but they were still based on the original concept. Among the new ideas were 12-volt electrics, electronic ignition, big-bore kits, engine tuning using current techniques, and massive drum brakes to ensure the right image. They may have differed in many details, but not from the initial idea.

Triumph

The Triumph range for 1960 was a mixture of old and new, for it included models that were direct descendants of the original pre-war Speed Twin, newer unit-construction twins and a new scooter range. Small motorcycles were exemplified by the Cub model in two forms. It added up to a successful list, which the company was to sell well throughout the decade, with suitable amendments to meet or set trends.

The scooters were three in number and exactly the same as the Sunbeam models in the BSA list, except for colour and badges. The Triumph versions were called Tigress and comprised the 172 cc two-stroke TS1, the 249 cc twin-cylinder TW2 and the TW2S, which had the electric starter. All were finished in Shell Blue sheen, a popular Meriden colour.

The single-cylinder Tiger Cubs came in two forms; the standard T20 and the sports T20S. Both had very similar engines based on the original 149 cc Terrier unit of 1952. The Cub engine was of 199 cc, both bore and stroke being increased from the Terrier dimensions to retain their near-square relationship. The four-speed gearbox was built in unit with the engine, both primary and final drives being on the left, while the gear lever and kickstart pedal were on the right.

The Cub engine had an inclined, cast-iron barrel and light-alloy cylinder head containing its two valves. The crankcase was unusual in that its vertical split line was not on the cylinder centre line but to the left, so the joint face was just inboard of the main bearing and the gearbox sprocket. Thus, the crankshaft and the gearbox were mainly contained by the major part of the crankcase.

On the left, the crankcase was sealed by the inner chaincase, which carried the drive-side main, a ball race, and was extended back to shield the gearbox sprocket. On the right, a similar full-length casting enclosed the timing gears, the oil pump, the gearbox and part of the selector mechanism. An outer cover sealed off the rest of this and gave the unit a smooth exterior, which was matched on the left by another outer cover.

The crankshaft ran in a plain timing-side main and was built up with a plain big-end. Spur gears drove the camshaft, and skew gears the points cam and oil pump. The pushrods moved in a separate tube (in typical Triumph fashion), and the rocker box was cast in one with the head. Pressed-steel covers sealed the box.

The camshafts differed between the two engines, as did the pistons, cylinder heads and valve springs. The T20S also had wide-ratio gears, but otherwise the two engine units were the same. The compression ratios were 7:1 for the T20 and 9:1 for the sports model. In both cases, the oil pump was a twin-plunger type similar to that used by Triumph for many years, and the top of its drive shaft was coupled to the ignition contact-breaker assembly. This, together with the advance mechanism, was contained in a small housing behind the cylinder, usually referred to as the

distributor, although it was simply a points housing.

The points assembly differed between the two models in respect of cam and spring set, as the road model had normal coil ignition, while the sports machine had energy transfer and a special coil, being very sensitive to points gap and ignition timing. Both models had an alternator on the left with a common rotor, but they had different stators.

Primary drive was by duplex chain to a three-plate clutch with a shock absorber built into its centre. The gearbox was of conventional British

Below left **Triumph Tigress, when launched at Earls Court late in 1958**

Right **Henry Cooper on a 1961 T20S/L Sports Cub at the Earls Court Show**

Below **This was President Kennedy's escort when he visited London in 1961. Naturally, the machines are Triumphs**

Above **The Triumph Tiger 110 in its final 1961 year, with bathtub**

Above left **The 1961 TR6 Trophy, which had changed from a trail bike to road model that year**

Left **Smallest 1961 twin was this Twenty-One, or model 3TA**

form, the gears being selected by a pair of forks moved by a quadrant form of cam-plate. The wider gear ratios were obtained by changing the sleeve gear and its layshaft mate alone. On the T20, a cable linked the cam-plate to a mechanical gear indicator mounted on the fork nacelle. A rack-and-pinion turned a pointer as required.

The engine unit was installed in a single-loop frame with a bolted-on subframe and pivoted-fork rear suspension. It was held at three points, and the exhaust system was on the right. That of the T20 ran at low level, but the T20S had its system at waist height. The silencers differed, that of the T20 being fitted with a mute for 1960. The carburettors also varied, with an 18 mm Zenith on the T20 and a Monobloc for the T20S.

Differences increased in the cycle parts, and there were far fewer common items compared with the engine unit. The T20 followed the Triumph trend for non-sporting models in having a degree of rear enclosure. This was not as extensive as on the larger models, covering a triangle framed

by the dualseat, seat tube and subframe tube. Each side panel or skirt was pierced, that on the right for the oil tank and that on the left for the toolbox.

The T20 had front forks modelled on the other machines in the range, with a nacelle for the headlamp. They were telescopic and had their seal surfaces protected by tubular extensions to the base of the nacelle, rather than by gaiters. Both wheels had 'sensible' mudguards, 17 in. rims and $5\frac{1}{2}$ in. brakes of the single-leading-shoe type.

The T20S had a sporting appearance, dispensing with the skirt and having a small toolbox and D-shaped air cleaner. The rear chainguard was much less enveloping, and the mudguards were slimmer with tubular stays at the front. The hubs were the same size, but the wheels were bigger— 19 in. at the front and 18 in. at the rear.

Forks were based on those used on the 350 cc twin, so they were heavier. They were fitted with gaiters and had neither nacelle nor lugs on the shrouds to support a headlamp. Where this was required, suitable shrouds with eyes were installed, and a small lamp shell used. This carried both the lights and switches. The system was direct, so no battery was fitted.

The tank and its badges differed from those of the T20, as did the dualseat and the oil tank. Unlike the standard model, the sports machine had an optional speedometer, but in all cases this was driven from the rear wheel.

The two Cub models experienced a major

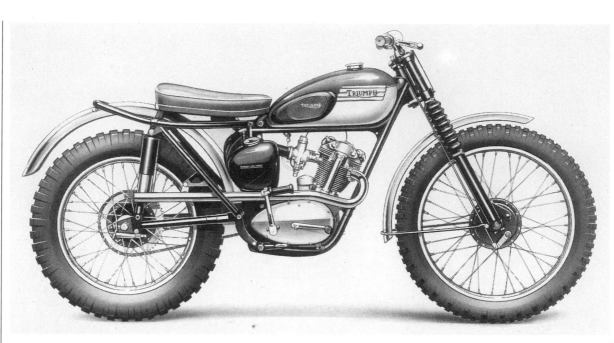

change to the engine early in 1960, which left the mechanics as they were, but moved the crankcase joint line to the centre of the cylinder. The castings were completely new, but they followed the lines of the older versions, retaining the complete gearbox shell in the right half. Despite the change, it was still necessary to split the case to get at the gearbox sprocket.

Next in the 1960 Triumph range were the unit-construction twins produced in 349 and 490 cc sizes. The design had appeared in 1957 in the smaller engine size as the model Twenty-One, and in time this became listed as the 3TA. By 1960 it had been joined by the very similar 5TA, which had a 490 cc engine, and for 1960 the sports T100A appeared in this larger size.

The engine design was in the classic Edward Turner mould, with 360-degree crankshaft, twin gear-driven camshafts placed fore and aft, and a twin-plunger oil pump. The crankcase was split on its centre line with the entire gearbox shell in the right half. The left half extended back as the inner section of the primary chaincase, but for this engine had an access hole for the gearbox sprocket. On the right, there were separate timing and inner and outer gearbox covers, which were shaped to blend into one. Inside, there was a one-piece crankshaft with bolted-on flywheel, drive-side ball race and timing-side bush for the mains, and plain big-ends for the connecting rods. The camshafts were driven by spur gears, the oil pump being operated from the inlet-cam gear nut.

The same camshaft also had a skew gear to drive the ignition cam through an advance mechanism, which was housed in a unit with the distributor behind the block. In this case, there really was a distributor in the assembly, so it was correctly named.

The block was of cast iron and the head light alloy with separate rocker boxes in Triumph fashion. Also typically Triumph were the pushrod tubes fore and aft of the block and the caps that gave access to the overhead-valve adjusters. The engine featured dry-sump lubrication, a single Amal Monobloc carburettor, and a low-level exhaust system on each side.

A conventional four-speed gearbox was installed, with right-hand gear pedal and kickstarter. It was driven by a multi-plate clutch, which was connected to the engine by a duplex primary chain. At that time, there was no tensioner for the chain on the 3TA model, although one was fitted to the larger versions. An alternator was mounted in the chaincase on the left-hand end of the crankshaft.

The 3TA frame comprised a single loop with duplex tubes under the engine unit and a bolted-on subframe. It had pivoted-fork rear suspension and telescopic front forks with a nacelle for the headlamp and combined lighting and coil-ignition switch. Both wheels had 17 in. rims, the front having a 7 in. brake in a full-width drum. At the rear, an offset hub with 7 in. brake was used. A quickly detachable hub was also available.

Above **Tiger 100SS from 1962, with skirt in place of the tourer's bathtub**

Above left **The 1962 Triumph TS20 Cub scrambler, which had dreadful energy-transfer ignition**

From its inception, the 3TA had promoted the idea of weather protection, concealed mechanics and a touring image. In part, this came from its well-valanced front mudguard, but in the main it was due to its rear enclosure. This extended from the carburettor to the rear number plate, but it left the hub on view. From the side, it had the appearance of an old-fashioned hip bath, stood upside-down, and it was immediately christened the Triumph bathtub. On top of the enclosure was a hinged dualseat, beneath which was a moulded rubber tray for the toolkit.

The 5TA was almost a replica of the 3TA with a larger bore and bigger carburettor. Internally, there were detail changes to suit the larger engine, but externally it was the red paint that was the easiest way of telling them apart, as the 3TA came in Shell Blue. Otherwise, only the fatter rear tyre helped, as nearly all the cycle parts were common.

The same applied to much of the black and ivory T100A, which had the 490 cc engine with high-compression pistons and different camshafts. The ignition was by energy transfer, so the stator and distributor differed, as did the light switch. There was an extra plate in the clutch to

cope with the added power, but just about all the cycle parts were the same.

The final quartet of machines belonged to an older generation of engine design. They were all of 649 cc with twin cylinders and overhead valves. The basic tourer was the Thunderbird 6T, and its sports version was the Tiger 110 or T110. This was developed further into a super-sports model known as the T120 Bonneville. Finally, there was the Trophy TR6, which was in the off-road style laid down by its 499 cc predecessor.

All these machines had a separate engine and gearbox assembly that had its roots in the original pre-war Speed Twin. It was not really much different from the small unit-construction twins, other than in the form of the crankcase halves. These still met on the engine centre line and carried a one-piece crankshaft with bolted-on flywheel. This assembly turned in a pair of ball races and had plain big-ends.

The timing side was the same as on the unit engines, with a gear drive to the camshafts, but in this case it was extended to the rear to drive a distributor on the 6T or a magneto on the other models. All had an alternator on the left, and the same arrangements for oil pump and valve gear. The block was cast in iron, but only the 6T had a cylinder head in the same material. That of the T110 and TR6 was in light alloy, as was the T120's, which differed in having splayed inlet-port stubs fitted to it. That model alone had twin carburettors, which were Monoblocs with

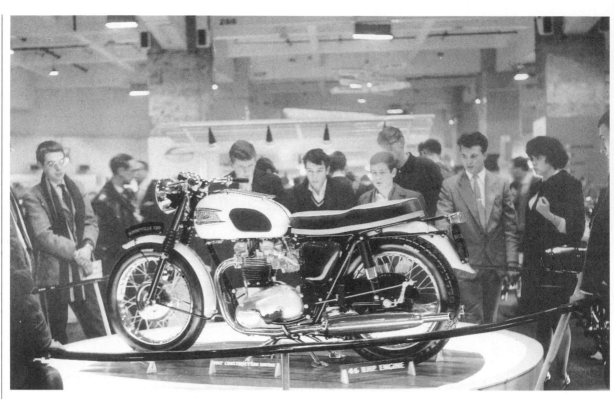

chopped-off float chambers. They were supplied from a separate, central, racing-style chamber that was rubber mounted.

A cast-alloy chaincase on the left took the power through a multi-plate clutch to a four-speed gearbox. This was in the normal Triumph style, but it had one unusual feature in the form of the Slickshift gear-change. With this, the rider did not need to use the clutch when changing gear, as the positive-stop mechanism was arranged to lift the clutch when the pedal was moved. It was not to everyone's liking and was not fitted on the T120.

The exhaust system of the TR6 was of the siamezed variety, the two pipes joining on the left at waist level to feed into a single silencer. The other three models had a low-level system on each side.

All the 650s had the same frame, which was new for 1960 and had duplex down-tubes running under the engine and gearbox. There was a single top tube, but after a short time a further bracing tube was added beneath it. The subframe was bolted to the main loop, and a pivoted rear fork provided the rear suspension.

The same basic telescopic forks were used by all, but on the 6T and T110 a nacelle carried the instruments and switches. The TR6 and T120 had forks with gaiters, a separate headlamp shell and a light switch positioned under the seat nose.

All models had a full-width front hub with a single-leading-shoe brake, which was 7 in. in size for the 6T and 8 in. for the rest. The machines had the same offset rear hub with 7 in. brake, or a similar quickly-detachable version. Wheel sizes were 18 in. for the 6T and T110, 19 in. for the T120, and one of each for the TR6, the larger one being at the front.

The 6T and T110 had the bathtub rear enclosure of the smaller unit twins, and although they had the hinged dualseat, there was no moulded rubber toolpad. Thus, other than the alloy head, larger front brake and markings, there was little to distinguish one model from another.

The TR6 and T120 dispensed with the bathtub, as they were built in a more sporting style. Their front mudguards were slimmer, and the oil tank and toolbox were designed to fit in with the sporting theme. The TR6 rear mudguard was shorter to suit its off-road purpose.

There were few changes for 1961, and for the scooters they amounted to additional colours and the option of a two-tone scheme. The T20 continued, but the T20S was replaced by two models. One was the T20T, which was aimed at trials use and was very similar to the earlier model. The other was the T20S/L which, while cast in much the same mould, was refined for enduro use. Thus, it retained its lights and had a higher compression ratio, sports camshaft and close-ratio gearbox. An optional rev-counter was driven from the end of the camshaft and called for a special timing cover, into which a skew-gear drive was assembled.

There was little change to the unit-construction twins, but they were joined by a more sporting model, which was listed as the T100SS. This differed from the T100A in having a rear skirt that was similar to the Tiger Cub's instead of the bathtub. It also had gaitered forks, a separate headlamp shell without a nacelle, and sports mudguards. Ball-ended clutch and brake levers were options.

Among the 650s, the 6T was fitted with the T110 light-alloy cylinder head, and the two Tiger models continued, but not the TR6 at first. This was dropped in the autumn of 1960 and did not reappear until early in 1961, when it took a new form. Essentially, it became a single-carburettor Bonneville, but it retained the Trophy name.

For 1962 the scooters remained as they were,

but the Cubs entered a period of revision, which began with the disappearance of the T20T and redesignation of the T20S/L as the T20S/S. In this form, it was hardly changed, but it was available with a low-compression engine for trials use.

Early in the new year the T20S/S was replaced on the home market by the T20S/H, but it continued for export. With the new machine came two special models, the TR20 for trials and TS20 for scrambles. All three, together with the T20S/S, had revised engine internals, the timing-side main becoming a ball race and the oil feed to the big end being revised. Ignition for the T20S/H was by coil, although the two competition models retained the energy-transfer system. Its cycle side had a sporting appearance, so it kept the front fork gaiters and did not have any rear enclosure. The competition machines were modified to suit their purpose, having different gear ratios, a short seat, alloy mudguards and stronger footrests.

The 3TA and 5TA switched to a siamezed exhaust system with the silencer low down on the right, while the T100A was dropped, so only the T100SS continued. This also had a siamezed

Above left **The first unit-construction Triumph Bonneville was this 1963 model, here being coveted**

Below **The Trials Cub, or TR20, of 1965, with camshaft points, which greatly improved matters**

exhaust. The 650s carried on without the T110 or the Slickshift mechanism in the gearbox, and both the 6T and TR6 were fitted with a siamezed exhaust.

In March 1962 there was a new addition to the range in the form of a small scooter. This was the Tina, which had a 100 cc two-stroke engine with fan cooling. The engine was installed so that the cylinder was horizontal, and it drove the rear wheel by V-belt. Incorporated in the front pulley were moving flanges which allowed the ratio to alter and acted as an automatic gearbox and clutch.

The engine and transmission assembly was hung from the main frame beam and formed the rear pivoted arm of the suspension. A single spring-and-damper unit controlled it, while at the front there was a single trailing arm controlled by rubber bushes, which provided the suspension. The wheels had pressed-steel, 8 in. split rims and 5 in. brakes.

The bodywork was of the usual scooter form, having an apron, floor and rear section with the seat on top. The front mudguard turned with the wheel. A good range of accessories was offered for the model.

It continued in this form for 1963 together with the other scooters, but there were more noticeable changes to the motorcycles. In essence, these comprised a change of points position for the Cub and some unit-twin models, a new sports 350, and a move to unit construction for the big twins.

The Cub range remained the same, and the T20 engine was given the ball-race timing main and the internal changes common to the other models. All, including the T20, finally dispensed with the points housing behind the cylinder, the points being moved to a housing in the timing cover. There, the advance mechanism and the points cam could be easily driven from the end of the camshaft, and this alteration did a great deal to ease the problems experienced with the energy-transfer system.

Further changes were the fitting of finned rocker covers in place of the old pressed-steel versions, and on the road models replacement of the gear indicator dial with a plunger. This rose out of the gearbox casting to show the ratio in use.

The same change to the points drive was made on the T100SS, using the exhaust camshaft. This model was joined by the 349 cc Tiger 90, which was built along the same lines, with a rear skirt and siamezed exhaust system. The touring 3TA and

Right **The TR6 Trophy in its earlier off-road form, and here prepared for Bud Ekins to ride in the ISDT**

Below **Triumph T100SS for 1965, by which time it had lost its skirt**

5TA models retained the older distributor ignition system, but they reverted to twin low-level exhaust pipes and silencers.

The three 649 cc models took on unit construction by adopting a similar design to the smaller unit engines. The gearbox shell was cast as part of the right-hand crankcase half, and the points were set into the timing cover. Many internal parts stayed the same, but this alteration gave the assembly a sleeker appearance.

Cycle parts reflected the trend away from enclosure, the 6T receiving the skirt from the small sports twins, but reverting to twin exhaust systems. The other two models continued in their more sporting image, the TR6 retaining the siamezed system, and the T120 its twin carburettors. Both had gaitered forks and a separate headlamp shell as before.

The entire range continued for 1964, the scooters and Cubs being unchanged. The 3TA and 5TA gained points in the timing chest and lost the bathtub. In its place, they had the sports model skirt, which was dispensed with on the T90 and T100SS. The last two were given twin exhaust systems, and all four models had new forks, although the tourers retained the nacelle. The new forks also appeared on the 650s, of which the 6T was given 12-volt electrics and the TR6 twin exhaust systems.

During 1964 the 249 cc twin-cylinder scooter

was dropped together with the TS20 scrambles Cub. The rest of the range continued for 1965 with an addition in the form of a high-performance T120. This was the Thruxton Bonneville, which was built with a fairing, rearsets and other useful parts from the list of options for production racing. It remained in the lists for six months only, as such a machine could be built up by any owner, using the optional parts offered by Triumph, and no two people's ideas on what was best were the same.

The other models carried on with little change for 1965, until the middle of the year. Then, the 172 cc scooter was dropped, while the Tina was restyled and renamed the T10. It had the same mechanics, but the panelling was altered and there were some detail changes.

The main Cub models remained, but the T20S/S was joined by a yellow trail version, which was sold in the USA as the Mountain Cub. The colour was to ensure recognition off-road and prevent shooting accidents, which did happen with other colours.

For 1966 the T10 continued as it was, but the T20 was given a change in cycle parts. These became more like those of the BSA Bantam—both had shared fork legs and wheel hubs for some time. Now the Cub lost its rear skirt and nacelle, but it gained the Bantam frame and headlamp shell, the former being modified to suit the engine mountings. The oil tank was styled to match the Bantam centre panels, and the wheel size was changed to 18 in. The mudguards were also taken from the BSA, but the petrol tank remained a Triumph unit.

The 3TA and 5TA lost their rear skirts for 1966 and were given 18 in. wheels and 12-volt electrics. This change also applied to the T90 and T100. The latter replaced the T100SS and was built in three forms, the basic T100 being the sports 490 cc model for general use. The other models were intended for the USA and were the T100C and T100R. Of these, the T100C was a trail bike, rather on the lines of the original TR models. It came in Eastern and Western forms. The differences

between these were the light-alloy mudguards fitted for the West Coast, and a variation in dualseat top colour, which was black in the east and grey elsewhere.

Otherwise, the T100C followed the lines of older trail models, having a siamezed exhaust running waist high on the left, 19 in. front wheel and direct lighting. The T100R was built as a street scrambler, so it was the same as the T100C, but with low-level exhausts and a full lighting set.

The 650 range was also extended for 1966, when the 6T lost its rear skirt, and extra models of the TR6 and T120 appeared for the USA. Like all the other models, they had new tank badges, but there were no other major alterations. The extra models were on the lines of the T100 machines, with an Eastern and Western version of the TR6C and a TR6R street model.

The Eastern TR6C was a street scrambler with direct lighting and a waist-level exhaust pipe and silencer on each side. The petrol tank was smaller than that of the standard model and the

Above **Triumph Super Cub of 1967, with full-width hubs, and in its final form**

Below **The 1968 T100C model, built for trail and enduro use in the USA**

Above **Triumph Daytona T100T from 1969, with twin-leading-shoe brake and two carburettors**

mudguards differed. Otherwise, there was little to distinguish it, other than the studded front tyre, smaller headlamp and high-rise bars.

The Western TR6C was much more of a scrambles machine, having no lights and open exhaust pipes, both of which ran at waist level on the left. Tyres were to suit off-road use, as was the addition of a sump plate, but the rest of the machine incorporated many stock road-model parts. It did have a smaller gearbox sprocket to lower the ratios, but it had the same compression ratio.

The TR6R was similar to the Eastern model, but it was for street use and had low-level exhausts and silencers. The headlamp was full size, so except for the high bars and lack of number plates it was the same as the stock model.

Following the same path was the T120R, an American street model with high bars and a small petrol tank. Otherwise, it was the standard Bonneville. The T120TT, however, was much further removed. This was a track racer with an 11:1 compression ratio, small tank, no lights and open exhaust pipes tucked in under the engine unit. It made a purposeful-looking machine.

There were more revisions for 1967, but not to the T10, except that its weathershield panels became detachable. The T20S/H, TR20, 3TA, 5TA

Above **Triumph TR25W of 1968, which was a badged BSA Starfire modified for off-road use**

Right **Very nice Trident parked above Ramsey in the Isle of Man. Not a standard front brake, but travelling marshals do have to travel**

and 6T all came to an end around the middle of 1966, so that 1967 range had a very sporting appearance, with the exception of the scooter and Cub. The last became the T20S/C Super Cub, but the only changes were to full-width hubs and the fitting of a Bantam tank.

The T90 continued as it was, but the T100 range was altered to four models. Both the T100C and T100R carried on, but the former was no longer built in Eastern and Western forms. The single machine had twin pipes and silencers running waist high on the left. It also had a new seat, which was common to the twin range, although the colour of its top panel varied on some models.

The T100R became more of a pure street bike for 1967, as the front tyre was changed to a ribbed section and the engine was modified to increase its power. It was fitted with twin carburettors, higher-compression pistons, a new cylinder head with splayed inlets, and a different exhaust camshaft.

On the home market, the T100 became the T100S and was joined by the T100T Daytona model. This had the twin-carburettor engine from the R model in the S cycle parts, producing a very-high-performance 500. The 650 models continued much as they were, the TR6C being built in one version only, but with twin waist-level exhaust systems on the left.

The arrival of 1968 brought Concentric carburettors on the twins, but there were no changes to the T10 or the Cub. The twin-carburettor 490 cc models were given an 8 in. front brake, but both TR6 and T120 switched to twin-leading-shoe operation at the front. Only these two 649 cc models remained, as the others had been dropped from the list. The T90 and two single-carburettor T100s continued.

There was one new model for 1968; the 247 cc TR25W. While this was a new single for Triumph, it was simply a badge-engineered BSA Starfire, which had been altered a little for trail use. Thus, the all-alloy engine unit was from the B25 and had a single cylinder, plain big end, unit construction and four-speed gearbox. As this engine was based on the C15 which, in turn, was derived from the Triumph Terrier and Cub, the wheel had turned full circle.

The cycle parts were mainly BSA items, although the forks came from the T90, but by that time many components were group inspired and used on both marques. The steel tank was Triumph, while the tyres were to suit trail use. In similar vein, a waist-level exhaust was tucked in behind the frame on the right, and a small headlamp was fitted.

During the year the Cub finally came to an end, but the rest of the range continued for 1969 with little alteration. This is not to say that there was no real news, for there was one new machine; the three-cylinder Trident T150. This mirrored the BSA Rocket 3, being for export only during 1968, but it came on to the home market in the following year.

The Trident was very similar to the BSA, but not quite the same, as its cylinders were mounted vertically, which required different crankcases. In addition, the timing side and gearbox end covers were altered in style to be separate items, as opposed to the BSA versions which flowed together. On the cycle side, a Bonneville-type frame was used, unlike the BSA's duplex version, but the forks, wheels and most other details were the same. The tank and side-cover details were unique to the marque, as were the seat and front mudguard.

During 1969 the T90 was dropped, as were the T100C and T100R at the end of that year. Both the T10 and TR25W continued for 1970, but in the case of the former only until the middle of the year, while the latter was replaced at the end of the year. The same happened to the T100S and T100T, but in their case the changes for 1971 were much less dramatic. In effect, the T100S became the T100C, a single-carburettor street scrambler, and the T100T became the T100R. These were, of course, the old American type numbers and reflected the firm's concern with that market.

The TR6 and T120 went through a similar change, but also had the infamous frame for 1971, which raised the seat height excessively. There were many other alterations, and prior to this major upheaval, the 1970 models had experienced few changes. This applied to the T150 which also remained as it was for 1970, but received a face-lift for the following year.

Thus, the Triumph range for the 1970s differed a good deal from that of 1960, and it was to experience some stormy times during the next decade-and-a-half.

Trobike

Trobike was one of the early makes of mini-bike and also one of the earliest to be sold in kit form to avoid purchase tax. It came from the Trojan works in Croydon, Surrey, where the firm also built go-karts and imported Lambretta scooters.

The Trobike was motorcycling reduced to its most basic elements, and for power it had a single-cylinder, 94 cc Clinton two-stroke engine. This had a cast-iron barrel, alloy head, recoil starter and fan cooling. The transmission comprised an automatic clutch and partly-enclosed chain. The fuel tank was part of the engine package and carried a petroil mixture for lubrication, while ignition was by flywheel magneto.

The engine was bolted into a simple frame, which was welded up as two loops. There was no suspension, other than the fat 5 in. tyres. The brakes were also 5 in. and operated by hand levers. A seat was bolted to the frame, and there were front and rear mudguards and a footrest bar. That was it.

In fact, there were two models, the Garden version being supplied without a front brake or number plates, which the road model retained. Originally, its main use had been on airfields and large industrial sites, but it soon spread to other areas where a short-hop machine was useful. With a top speed of about 30 mph, a trip of a mile or so became much quicker than walking. A machine out of the mainstream, the Trobike was still a feature in 1960, and for a few years after.

Trobike in the Isle of Man, in 1960

Velocette

In 1960 Velocette were following two distinct lines with their range of machines. Smallest in capacity and number of models were those based on their post-war, side-valve flat twin, while the rest, larger both in range size and capacity, had roots in the pre-war MOV model of 1933. This had been followed by the MAC and MSS machines in larger capacities, establishing the ohv M-series which, in time, replaced the more expensive K-series of overhead-camshaft models.

The small flat twin was the LE which, by 1960, had become the 192 cc MkIII model, but it was still very much in the image of the original 1949 machine. Changes to the MkIII had brought a four-speed gearbox with footchange and kickstarter, but the engine retained its side valves and water cooling. It had a built-up crankshaft, iron barrels and alloy heads, the valves being in the upper part of the barrel. The camshaft was above the crankshaft and gear driven from it, while the alternator and points were on the crankshaft nose.

Lubrication was by wet sump, the oil being carried in a pan attached to the underside of the main crankcase casting and circulated by a single gear-type pump through an external filter. The carburettor was a Monobloc, which replaced the earlier multi-jet instrument, and the cooling system was pure thermo-syphon without pump or thermostat. The silencer box was mounted under the gearbox, where the pipe from each cylinder joined it, and it had a single outlet.

The engine had primary drive gears behind it which drove the clutch. This, in turn, passed the power to the gearbox, which was of the cross-over, all-indirect type, so the drive came in on one shaft at the front, and went out on the other at the

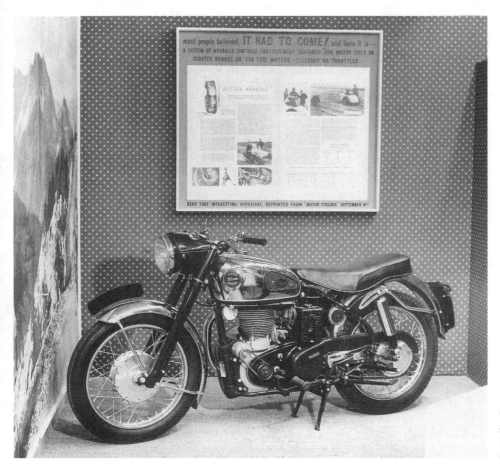

Velocette single, on show in 1959, minus its dynamo belt cover and left side cowling

back. Final drive was by enclosed shaft, which ran down the left leg of the rear pivoted fork to the bevel box in the rear wheel hub.

Engine, gearbox and rear fork were designed as a complete assembly, which could be detached as such from the main frame. The latter was one of the distinctive features of the machine and was formed from steel pressings, from which the power unit was suspended. A stowage compartment was incorporated in the top, with the petrol tank behind it and contained within the frame. The saddle also sat above the main pressing, which was continued to the rear as a huge mudguard.

At the front, the machine had telescopic forks and another massive mudguard, while both wheels were 18 in. with 5 in. brakes in full-width hubs. The headlamp shell carried the speedometer and switches, being cowled to the forks. Weather protection was enhanced by built-in legshields, which were joined to footboards that ran back for both rider and passenger. The latter sat on either a pad or the rear half of an optional dualseat.

The LE was an unusual machine and not easily classified, but the Valiant, which was derived from it, was much more conventional. For all that, it was still quite different from the average 200 cc machine built in Britain, as most were two-strokes or singles.

The Valiant differed from the LE in having air cooling, overhead valves and a tubular cradle frame. However, it had the same capacity, layout, gears, final drive and suspension systems. Essentially, the engine was the same as the MkIII, other than the top halves, pistons and camshaft plus a number of detail modifications made to suit the new installation.

The frame had a single top tube, but duplex tubes elsewhere, with the LE telescopics and rear fork. The mudguards had a more sporting appearance, but the wheels remained the same as on the LE, and the other fittings followed normal motorcycle lines. The entire engine assembly was enclosed by a two-piece cowl, but this left the heads and cylinders out in the air. Each head had its own carburettor, and there was a separate exhaust system on each side.

In addition to the Valiant, Velocette offered the Valiant Veeline. This was a standard Valiant complete with a dolphin fairing that had a bonded-in fascia panel, glove box and wide windscreen. Otherwise, it was the same model.

The rest of the range comprised ohv singles, all cast in the same mould and all but one with the same stroke. The exception was the 349 cc MAC, which had the 68 mm bore of the original MOV with a long 96 mm stroke. Construction was

typical of the M-series and characteristic of Velocette. The engine's design was based on a narrow crankcase, in which the main bearings were brought in as close as possible to be directly under the loads on them. Much of the success and long-term reliability of Velocette engines came from their use of a very stiff, well-supported crankshaft assembly. This was supplemented by arranging the primary chain to run close in to the engine which, in turn, led to the unusual, and much famed, Velocette clutch with the gearbox sprocket mounted outboard of it. This set-up played its part in keeping the loads close to the bearings which, as a result, could be kept small and light without any danger of overloading.

The engine also featured a high camshaft and very short pushrods, all on its right-hand side. The camshaft was driven through an idler and, in turn, drove the magneto gear. All the timing gears had helical teeth, and the idler could be moved a little to set the mesh, ensuring quiet running without

Below left **Velocette Valiant, sectioned to show all the workings of the mechanics**

Below **The LE model, as it was in 1960, with foot-change and a kickstarter**

gear whine. A pair of cam followers moved the pushrods, which ran in a single tube. The magneto gear nut was used to drive a rev-counter gearbox, which was bolted to the outside of a special timing cover. The cover, drive and instrument were an option and could be used on most models if required.

The top half comprised a separate cylinder and head with a large rocker box incorporating a side cover to give access to the rocker-arm adjusters at the tops of the pushrods. There was an exhaust-valve lifter with external lever in the top corner of the timing chest, and oil-feed and rocker drain pipes, which were very much in the Velocette image.

Lubrication was by dry sump, a double-gear pump being fitted at the bottom of the crankcase and driven from the crankshaft. The magneto was tucked in behind the cylinder, while the dynamo was clamped to the front of the crankcase and driven by a belt.

The engine was installed with its cylinder vertical, the primary chain passing its power to the narrow Velocette clutch. This is the subject of much lore, but in fact it is fairly normal, other than in its use of a multiplicity of small springs rather than three or four large ones. However, plate distortion can cause problems because the

assembly is too narrow to accommodate this and still have enough room to free off cleanly.

The real difference lies in the clutch lift mechanism and its adjustment, any wear or play having a noticeable effect on the settings, which are critical. Clearances must be minimal or the clutch will not free, but if taken too far the internal lever comes up against the gearbox shell, the clearance vanishes and the pressure plate is lifted, causing the clutch to slip.

The gearbox was designed very much on British lines, other than in having the output sprocket outboard of the clutch. Inside, there were four sturdy pairs of gears and a disc cam-plate, while the gear pedal and kickstart lever were on the right.

All the frames had pivoted rear forks and were robustly built in traditional style with single top and down-tubes. The tops of the rear suspension units could be moved along curved slots to alter their angle and, thus, the effective spring stiffness. The front forks were telescopic with hydraulic damping and an offset wheel spindle.

There were detail differences from model to model, but most of these were to suit a particular use or to provide a variation in appearance, while retaining the major components. There was also a good option list, which ranged from such basic items as an air filter and a steering damper to full-width hubs, alloy rims and even an exhaust megaphone.

The MAC was the smallest and most basic model with a capacity of 349 cc and a low compression ratio for touring. The MSS was its 499 cc equivalent and, like all the singles except the MAC, had the 86 mm stroke. It retained the low compression ratio and had fairly heavy flywheels. For sports use, the ratios went up and the flywheel weight came down to produce the 350 cc Viper and 499 cc Venom. All had a cowl over the top of the headlamp shell for the instruments. The MSS and two sports models also had engine cowlings.

The cowlings were of fibreglass and ran from the front of the engine level with the crankcase top. A hole at the front let in cooling air for the dynamo. The lower panel edge ran along the bottom frame rail to the rear wheel where it was taken up at an angle. It continued back as far as the pillion rests, and on the left side was carried up to enclose the battery and, to some extent, the carburettor. A different line was followed on the right, where the panel ran along the base of the oil tank and then the toolbox.

The two sports models were joined by two more for 1960, being known as the Viper and Venom Clubman. In this form, no panels were fitted, so the

crankcase and gearbox castings were polished. In effect, both were the sports models fitted, as standard, with the desirable options from the list for clubman or production racing.

Thus, the engines came with a TT carburettor and racing magneto with manual control. The footrests were rearsets with pedals to suit, and a close-ratio gearbox was fitted. Power was increased by raising the compression ratio, and there were a lot of detail improvements in such areas as the petrol tank mounting and even the taps. Front forks with two-way damping were supplied together with a steering damper, ball-ended levers and low bars. A megaphone was

Above **Velocette Vogue with plastic body on LE mechanics, which few bought**

Above right **Very different Venom Special, with engine cowlings to enclose its entrails**

Right **Watch the counter and do not exceed 6200 rpm on this 1965 Venom Clubman Veeline**

available instead of the normal lozenge-shaped Velocette silencer with its fishtail. A rev-counter and alloy rims were further options.

The next pair of models were the 350 and 500 Scramblers with engines built to the Clubman standard in a lighter frame that had fixed rear suspension-unit tops. The forks with two-way damping were fitted together with a waist-level, open exhaust pipe, light-alloy mudguards, and suitable tyres and bars. A further off-road model was the Endurance, which was originally designed for the USA. It had the Venom engine and most of that machine's cycle parts, but with a 21 in. front wheel, sports tyres, high bars and small fuel tank. Full lighting equipment was retained to produce a machine that was equally at home on road or trail.

At the end of that season the MAC was dropped together with the Valiant Veeline, but there were five new models—four singles and a scooter. The LE and Valiant continued, as did the Viper and Venom (in standard and Clubman forms), the MSS, the two Scramblers and the Endurance. The four new singles were created by simply adding a dolphin fairing to the existing sports machines to produce Viper and Venom Veeline and Clubman Veeline models. All had a similar fairing with integral fascia panel for the instruments and switches plus a screen. The Clubman fairings were smaller than the standard versions, and the screens were shorter to match their intended use. These models continued without the side panels that were fitted to the others.

The scooter was the last really new machine Velocette were to produce, as other new models to come were simply variations on an existing theme. It came about because the firm's dealers were pressing for something to sell against the very

Left **A 1967 Thruxton Venom, the end result of the long development of the Velocette high-camshaft engine**

Below **A 1966 Viper during a road test, with Bob Currie aboard and enjoying the ride**

successful Lambretta and Vespa models, but Velocette, like most British firms, misjudged the reason for their success. They also failed to realize quite how much special machinery was being used to make Italian scooters on a really large scale and, consequently, at low cost.

Velocette made two other errors. One was timing, for 1961 was the year to move out of the scooter market and into small cars, for that was where the customers were going. The other was hardly a mistake but more a foible of Velocette; they could not do any job other than in a sound engineering manner. Sadly, this cut no ice with most scooter buyers, who sought style and neat lines with mechanics that were out of sight and mind.

The result was the Viceroy (not the best of names), which Hall Green built as an open-frame motorcycle. The engine was a flat twin to reduce vibration and a two-stroke to keep it simple and narrow. It was positioned just behind the front wheel for good weight distribution, and it was conventional enough, apart from having reed valves to let the gases into the crankcase. The crankshaft was pressed up on slow tapers, which

was normal practice for the firm, and carried the electrics on its nose with a starter ring at the rear. The starter motor was mounted on top of the crankcase, and the light-alloy heads and barrels were air-cooled.

The entire transmission was formed into one unit, which acted as the rear suspension pivot arm. It was driven by a short propellor shaft through universal-joint discs, and at the rear this was coupled to the clutch by a short duplex chain. Both clutch and four-speed gearbox were taken from the LE and were connected directly to the rear-wheel bevel gears.

The engine was suspended from a single, large frame tube, which rose at the front to the headstock, and at the rear to the top of the single spring-and-damper unit. The transmission unit was pivoted from frame brackets, and the fuel

Above right **The Velocette 349 cc Scrambler, with fixed rear units, that continued in limited production for most of the decade**

Below **1967 Venom Veeline, showing both the fairing and the engine cowl**

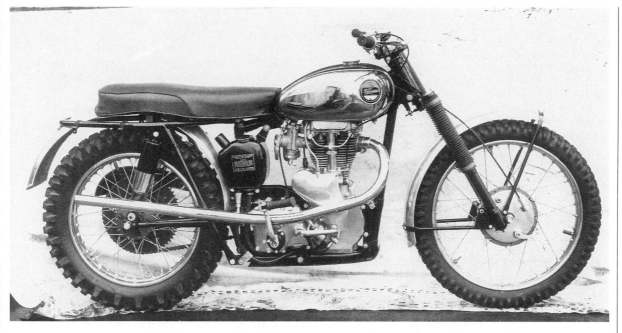

tank was above the engine and behind the headstock. The two batteries were concealed under the dualseat nose.

Telescopic front forks, based on those of the LE, were fitted, and both wheels were of the pressed-disc type. They were of 12 in. diameter and bolted to hubs with 6 in. brakes. A panel at the top of the forks carried the instruments and switches. The mechanics were covered by the body, which followed scooter convention, having an apron, floor, rear body and fixed front mudguard.

There were also panels over the fuel tank, and a second front mudguard was fixed to the forks to keep road dirt off the engine in general, and its electrics in particular. The floor behind the apron was not flat but had a noticeable tunnel to accommodate the propellor shaft. A windscreen was fitted as standard.

The machine was massive in appearance, especially when seen alongside the dainty Italian offerings, and this did nothing to help its sales. It also had some odd features and was rather noisy, so many customers were put off right away and never found out about its good performance and superior handling.

The Viceroy scooter was unchanged for 1962 when the entire range continued as it was, and it was nearly the same story for 1963. Two more singles were listed that year, being the Viper and Venom Specials, which were simply standard models with a plainer finish and reduced price.

During the year another new model appeared, but this was a flat-twin variant based on the LE and named the Vogue.

In essence, the newcomer was an LE with a fibreglass body and a new frame to support it. The mechanical side comprised the LE engine, gearbox and rear-fork assembly with few alterations. The front forks and both wheels also came from the LE, as did the radiator. The frame was new with a massive backbone linking the headstock to the rear subframe structure.

The main part of the body ran from the headstock to the rear number plate. It incorporated the petrol tank, and at the front there was another moulding which carried two headlamps mounted side-by-side. There were also legshields, a truly massive front mudguard, and side panels with the usual LE-style footboards. The dualseat sat on top of the body, and the machine had a windscreen.

The result had rather too much weight and bulk, so acceleration was poor and gradients proved a problem, but it offered good handling and was a very quiet motorcycle.

For 1964 the range continued as before, except that the two Scramblers and the Endurance models were available to special order only. During the year the Valiant was dropped, and at the end of the year the Viceroy was discontinued.

For 1965 the range was announced as before, with an extra in the form of an optional cylinder

head for the Venom Clubman. This had a bigger inlet valve, which was intended to be supplied by an Amal GP carburettor on a long inlet tract. To accommodate this, it needed an oil tank with a cut-away section. A modified fuel tank was also listed. At the other end of the scale, the LE was given 12-volt electrics, but the rest of the range remained as it was.

At the end of 1964 one further model joined the range. This was the Venom Thruxton, which came as standard with the new big-valve head, a GP carburettor, different oil tank and competition-style controls. Thus, it combined all the options that a rider would require for fast sports use or production racing, and it became the highlight of Velocette's big single range.

The full range of 17 models went forward for 1966, 12-volt electrics being added to the Vogue, but not much else altered. The Viper and Venom Clubman models in standard and Veeline forms took on a MkII guise. This amounted to the use of the Thruxton gaitered front forks with brackets for the headlamp shell, twin-leading-shoe front brake, a combined toolbox and battery container on the left, swept-back exhaust pipe and narrower mudguards. It all made for a more sporting image, which fitted in with the times.

Velocette had one great advantage over all the others, for their image was based on hard fact. This was the 24-hour world record, which they had taken in 1961 at just over 100 mph. A remarkable achievement, and while the unlimited-capacity record was to move on, the 500 cc class stayed with Velocette. It fitted in well with their solid,

reliable and very fast singles.

The same range was offered for 1968, but the day of the single, even the Velocette single, had passed, and performance seekers simply bought a 650 twin or one of the larger Japanese machines which were beginning to appear. Owners who respected the honest, fine engineering in the Velocette design and who would put up with its foibles grew fewer.

At the end of 1968 the range was reduced considerably to reflect these changes. The Vogue was dropped, as were all the Vipers and the Venom Special. This left the Venom (in standard, Clubman, Veeline and Clubman Veeline form), the Thruxton, the MSS and the LE. Also available for export were the 500 Scrambler and Endurance models.

The range continued for 1970, but by then the firm was in a poor trading condition, as machines were not selling. This brought the decision to go into voluntary liquidation early in 1971, the assets and tools being sold off so that all creditors could be paid in full. An honest end to an honest firm, run throughout its life by three generations of an honest family—the Goodmans.

Above **Thruxton Venom with big carburettor and tank cut away to clear it—very much an enthusiast's machine**

Left **Same big carburettor, but with high bars for the USA—not really the Velocette style**

Viscount

There were plenty of Tritons and specials with Triumph or other engines on the roads during the late 1950s and 1960s, but a few riders went one better. They scorned the vertical twin with its vibration, opting instead for the bigger V-twin of the 998 cc Vincent.

The idea of fitting one of these engines into a featherbed frame was attractive, and one of the earliest was built in Australia in 1953. Once it was known to be possible, others soon appeared, although it was never an easy job and always a tight squeeze. The package worked well as a road machine or for racing, but relatively few were built. Not only was it a difficult job, but a big Vincent engine was much more expensive than a 650 Triumph, nor was it so easy to obtain.

When Vincents stopped production, the practice began to die out as supplies diminished, but there was a brief revival of the idea in 1960. This came from a dealer who sought to build the machines on a limited-production basis and sell them as the Viscount.

The machine followed traditional lines for this form of special, with an all-welded wideline frame, Norton forks and a Manx front hub. Most of the cycle parts were Norton, suitably modified where necessary, and the engine was built to the Black Shadow standard.

The result was a very fast road machine, but inevitably the price was high and, thus, demand was low. Most riders preferred to buy a standard model from one of the major marques, rather than take on a special with an expensive engine made by a firm that no longer existed. Special enthusiasts preferred to assemble their own machines, rather than buy standard products, and the café-racer fraternity kept to the Goldie or a vertical twin.

So, few Viscounts were built,, and the idea lapsed once more as the market went its own way.

The Viscount with big V-twin Vincent engine shoe-horned into a Norton frame—very quick, very nice, but not a success

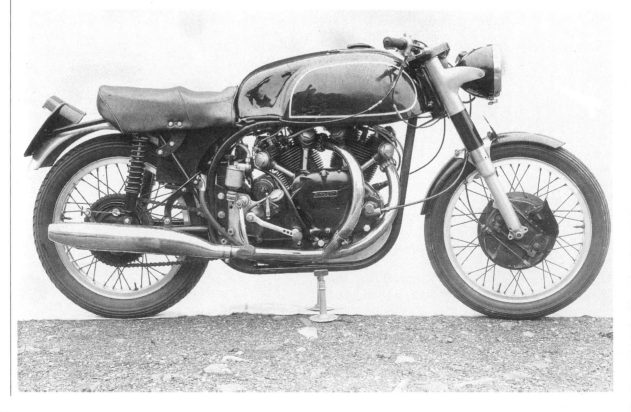

Wasp

The Wasp hailed from Wiltshire and was another case of a machine built as a special being successful enough to generate requests for duplicates. The original models were sidecar-racing outfits used on grass and in scrambles. In each case, they were fitted with trailing-link forks.

The forks worked well, but before taking up the orders for them, Wasp built some solo competition machines for trials and scrambles. These followed a classic pattern, having a Triumph twin engine, AMC gearbox, Norton forks and a full duplex frame. The engine unit was bolted directly into the frame without engine plates, and fibreglass was used for the petrol tank, seat pan, rear tail, side plates and air box.

The result was a tidy machine, not unlike the Rickman, and it was produced as a kit or a complete machine, the business being run on a part-time basis. Sidecar outfits followed, and at the end of the 1960s the firm went over to building sidecar scramblers full-time. They proved to be very good indeed, and Wasps with Triumph, Norton, BMW, Honda, Kawasaki, Yamaha and other engines ran so well that they took the European Sidecar Cross Championship for 1971. They continued to win this for a good few years, and carried on doing so after the event took on world status.

Never a road model, the Wasp was nonetheless a very successful competition machine.

Above **The Wasp factory, seen in 1977, with an interesting Vincent project in the centre**
Below **Wasp grass-track outfit with nickel-plated frame and Norton Atlas engine**

Model charts

The charts supplement the text to show how the manufacturers' ranges varied through the decade. Each list gives the range for each year, including models introduced during the year. Normally, the model year ran from about October of the previous calendar year, but by the late 1960s this practice had largely ceased.

Each chart shows the models, their capacity and engine type. The capacity is calculated from the bore and stroke, which is also given for many makes. Where a Villiers engine was used, its type number is given instead, and for some mopeds the name of the engine manufacturer only is shown. The model number or name is given under each year it was produced, with abbreviations where necessary. These are listed under each make.

The charts are arranged to run from the smallest to the largest model. Thus, sequences of a particular size of machine can be traced through the years. Referring back to the main text should help clarify any doubtful points.

AJS

	b × s	60	61	62	63	64	65	66	67	68	69	70
246 ts	66 × 72										37A-T	
247 ts	68 × 68									DT		
247 ts	68 × 68									Al	Y4	Y4
247 ts	68 × 68											Y40
368 ts	83 × 68											Y5
368 ts	83 × 68											Y50

Al – Alamos
DT – Double T

AMC – AJS

	b × s	60	61	62	63	64	65	66	67	68	69	70
248 ohv	70 × 65	14	14	14	14							
248 ohv	70 × 65	14CS	14CS	14CS								
248 ohv				14S	14S							
248 ohv				14CSR	14CSR	14CSR	14CSR	14CSR				
348 ohv	69 × 93	16	16									
348 ohv	69 × 93	16C	16C	16C	16C							
348 ohv	74 × 81			16	16							
348 ohv	74 × 81			16S								
348 ohv	72 × 85.5	8	8	8		16	16	16				
348 ohv	72 × 85.5					16C						
349 ohc	75.5 × 78	7R	7R	7R	7R							
497 ohv	82.5 × 93	18	18	18	18							
497 ohv	86 × 85.5					18	18	18				
497 ohv	86 × 85.5	18CS	18CS	18CS	18CS	18CS	18CS					
498 ohv twin	66 × 72.8	20	20									
646 ohv twin	72 × 79.3	31	31	31	31	31	31	31				
646 ohv twin	72 × 79.3	31dl	31dl									
646 ohv twin	72 × 79.3	31CS										
646 ohv twin	72 × 79.3	31CSR	31CSR	31CSR	31CSR	31CSR	31CSR	31CSR				
745 ohv twin	73 × 89						33	33	33			
745 ohv twin	73 × 89						33CSR	33CSR	33CSR			

Left **Show time was at Brighton, on the south coast, in September 1965. The industry also tried Blackpool in its hunt for customers**

Right **AJS 31CSR sports twin in Germany on a press trip**

AMC – MATCHLESS

248 ohv	b × s	60	61	62	63	64	65	66	67	68	69	70
248 ohv	70 × 65	G2	G2	G2	G2							
248 ohv	70 × 65	G2CS	G2CS	G2CS								
248 ohv	70 × 65			G2S	G2S							
248 ohv	70 × 65			G2CSR	G2CSR	G2CSR	G2CSR	G2CSR				
348 ohv	69 × 93	G3	G3									
348 ohv	69 × 93	G3C	G3C	G3C	G3C							
348 ohv	74 × 81			G3	G3							
348 ohv	74 × 81			G3S								
348 ohv	72 × 85.5	G5	G5	G5		G3	G3	G3				
348 ohv	72 × 85.5					G3C						
496 ohc	90 × 78	G50	G50	G50	G50							
496 ohc	90 × 78			G50CSR								
497 ohv	82.5 × 93	G80	G80	G80	G80							
497 ohv	86 × 85.5					G80	G80	G80				
497 ohv	86 × 85.5	G80CS	G80CS	G80CS	G80CS	G80CS	G80CS	G85CS	G85CS	G85CS	G85CS	
498 ohv twin	66 × 72.8	G9	G9									
646 ohv twin	72 × 79.3	G12	G12	G12	G12	G12	G12	G12				
646 ohv twin	72 × 79.3	G12dl	G12dl									
646 ohv twin	72 × 79.3	G12CS										
646 ohv twin	72 × 79.3	G12CSR	G12CSR	G12CSR	G12CSR	G12CSR	G12CSR	G12CSR				
745 ohv twin	73 × 89						G15	G15	G15	G15	G15	
745 ohv twin	73 × 89						G15CSR	G15CSR	G15CSR	G15CSR	G15CSR	
745 ohv twin	73 × 89								G15CS	G15CS	G15CS	
750 ohv twin				G15/45								

AJW

48 ts	Engine	60	61	62	63	64	65	66	67	68	69	70
48 ts	Min	FC	FC	FC	FC	FC						
48 ts	Min		G	G	G	G						
48 ts	Min		Vixen	Vixen	Vixen	Vixen						
49.7 ts	Min			SS	SS	SS						

FC – Fox Cub
G – Giulietta
Min – Minarelli
SS – Giulietta Super Sport

AMBASSADOR

	Engine	60	61	62	63	64	65	66	67	68	69	70
50 ts	3K			Moped								
174 ts	2L	Pop										
174 ts	3L		Sco	Sco								
197 ts	9E	3SS	3SS	3SS	3SS	3SS						
197 ts	9E			Pop								
249 ts twin	2T	SS	SS	SS	SS							
249 ts twin	4T					SS						
249 ts twin	2T		E75	E75	E75							
249 ts twin	4T					E75						
249 ts twin	2T		SSp	SSp	ST							

E75 – Electra 75   SSp – Super Sports
Pop – Popular   ST – Sports Twin
Sco – Scooter   3SS – 3-Star Special
SS – Super S

ARIEL

	b × s	60	61	62	63	64	65	66	67	68	69	70
48 ts	40 × 38											Ar3
50 ohv	38.9 × 42					Pi	Pi					
199 ts twin	48.5 × 54					200	200					
247 ts twin	54 × 54	Le	Le	Le	Le	Le	Le					
247 ts twin	54 × 54	Ar	Ar	Ar	Ar	Ar						
247 ts twin	54 × 54		SS	SS	SS	SS	SS					
646 ohv twin	70 × 84	Cy										

Ar – Arrow   Pi – Pixie
Ar3 – Ariel 3   SS – Super Sports
Cy – 650 Cyclone   200 – 200 Arrow
Le – Leader

BOND

	Engine	60	61	62	63	64	65	66	67	68	69	70
148 ts	31C	P3	P3	P3								
197 ts	9E	P4	P4	P4								

BSA

Model charts

	b × s	60	61	62	63	64	65	66	67	68	69	70
70 ts	45 × 44	Da	Da	Da								
75 ohv	47.6 × 42					K1	K1					
123 ts	52 × 58	D1	D1	D1	D1							
172 ts	61.5 × 58	D7	D7	D7	D7	D7	D7	D7/10	D10	D14	D175	D175
247 ohv	67 × 70	C15	C15	C15	C15	C15	C15	C15	C15		B25Fl	
247 ohv	67 × 70	C15S	C15S	C15S	C15S	C15S	C15S					
247 ohv	67 × 70	C15T	C15T	C15T	C15T	C15T	C15T					
247 ohv	67 × 70				C15P	C15P	C15P					
247 ohv	67 × 70		SS80	SS80	SS80	SS80	SS80	C15Sp	C25	B25	B25	B25
343 ohv	79 × 70		B40	B40	B40	B40	B40					
343 ohv	79 × 70			SS90	SS90	SS90	SS90					
343 ohv	79 × 70					B40E	B40E					
348 ohv	71 × 88	B32GS	B32GS	B32GS								
441 ohv	79 × 90						B44GP	B44GP	B44GP			
441 ohv	79 × 90							B44VE	B44VE			
441 ohv	79 × 90								B44VS	B44VS	B44VS	B44VS
441 ohv	79 × 90								B44VR	B44SS	B44SS	B44SS
499 ohv	85 × 88	B33										
499 ohv	85 × 88	B34GS	B34GS	B34GS	B34GS							
591 sv	82 × 112	M21	M21	M21	M21							
497 ohv twin	66 × 72.6	A7	A7	A7								
497 ohv twin	66 × 72.6	A7SS	A7SS	A7SS								
499 ohv twin	65.5 × 74			A50	A50	A50	A50	A50	A50	A50	A50	A50
499 ohv twin	65.5 × 74						A50C	A50W	A50W			
499 ohv twin	65.5 × 74					A50CC	A50CC					
646 ohv twin	70 × 84	A10	A10	A10	A10							
646 ohv twin	70 × 84	A10SR	A10SR	A10SR	A10SR							
646 ohv twin	70 × 84	Spit	Spit	Spit	Spit							
646 ohv twin	70 × 84			RGS	RGS							
654 ohv twin	75 × 74			A65	A65	A65	A65	A65T	A65T	A65T	A65T	A65T
654 ohv twin	75 × 74					A65R	A65R					
654 ohv twin	75 × 74					A65T/R	A65LC					
654 ohv twin	75 × 74					A65L/R	A65L/R	A65Sp	A65Sp	A65Sp		
654 ohv twin	75 × 74						A65L	A65L	A65L	A65L	A65L	A65L
654 ohv twin	75 × 74					A65SH	A65SH	A65H	A65H	A65FS	A65FS	A65FS
740 ohv triple	67 × 70									A75	A75	A75

Da – Dandy
Fl – Fleetstar
GS – Gold Star
P – Pastoral
RGS – Rocket Gold Star
Sp – Sportsman (C15)
   – Spitfire (A65)
Spit – Spitfire (A10)
SR – Super Rocket

Above left **BSA Rocket 3 posed with 1960s-style clothes, which could be painful in a fall**

Left **BSA twins due for dispatch to Venezuela, with extra equipment and an alternator to power it**

219

BUTLER

Engine		60	61	62	63	64	65	66	67	68	69	70
246 ts	32A					Tem	Tem	Tem				
246 ts	32A/P					Fury	Fury	Fury				
246 ts	36A					Spa	Spa	Spa				
246 ts	36A/P					Spi	Spi	Spi				
247 ts	Star					St	St	St				

/P – Parkinson top half   St – Star-rider
Spa – Spartan   Star – Starmaker
Spi – Spitfire   Tem – Tempest

COTTON

Engine		60	61	62	63	64	65	66	67	68	69	70
197 ts	9E	Tr	Tr	Tr	Tr							
197 ts	9E	Vu	Vu	Vu	Vu							
197 ts	9E	Vu Sp	Vu Sp	Vu Sp	Vu Sp	Vu Sp	Vu Sp	Vu Sp	Vu Sp			
242 ts twin	Anz	Cot										
246 ts	33A	Sc	Sc									
246 ts	34A		Sc	Sc								
246 ts	32A		Tr	Tr	Tr	Tr	Tr	Tr				
246 ts	37A								Tr	Tr		
246 ts	31A		Cor	Cor	Cor	Cor	Cor					
246 ts	34A/C			Cou								
246 ts	36A/P				Cou	Cou	Cou	Cou				
246 ts	32A/P				Tr Sp	Tr Sp	Tr Sp					
247 ts	Star				Cobra	Cobra	Cobra					
247 ts	Star				Tel	Tel	Tel	Tel	Tel			
247 ts	Star						St Tr	St Tr	St Tr			
247 ts	Star						Con	Con	Con	Con		
247 ts	Star							Co Sp	Co Sp	Coss		
249 ts twin	2T	Her	Her	Her	Her	Her	Her					
249 ts twin	2T	DG	DG	DG	DG							
249 ts twin	2T		Cont	Cont	Cont							
249 ts twin	2T				C Sp	C Sp						
249 ts twin	4T						C Sp	C Sp	C Sp			
322 ts twin	Anz	Cot										
324 ts twin	3T	Mes	Mes	Mes	Mes	Mes	Mes					

Anz – Anzani   Cot – Cotanza   Sc – Scrambler
/C – Cross top half   Cou – Cougar   Star – Starmaker
Con – Conquest   C Sp – Continental Sports   St Tr – Starmaker Trials
Cont – Continental   DG – Double Gloucester   Tel – Telstar
Cor – Corsair   Her – Herald   Tr – Trials
Co Sp – Cobra Special   Mes – Messenger   Tr Sp – Trials Special
Coss – Cossack   /P – Parkinson top half   Vu – Vulcan
   Vu Sp – Vulcan Sports

DAYTON

	Engine	60	61	62	63	64	65	66	67	68	69	70
174 ts	2L	AF										
246 ts	2H	ACSS										
249 ts twin	2T	ACS										

ACS – Albatross Continental Scooter
ACSS – Albatross Continental Single Scooter
AF – Albatross Flamenco

DKR

	Engine	60	61	62	63	64	65	66	67	68	69	70
148 ts	31C	Peg										
148 ts	31C	Dove										
148 ts	31C			Cap	Cap	Cap	Cap	Cap	Cap				
174 ts	2L		PII									
174 ts	2L			C dl	C dl	C dl	C dl	C dl	C dl				
174 ts	2L			C std	C std	C std	C std	C std	C std				
197 ts	9E	Def	Def										
197 ts	9E			200 dl	200 dl	200 dl	200 dl	200 dl				
197 ts	9E				200 st	200 st	200 st	200 st				
249 ts twin	2T	Manx	Manx										

Cap – Capella I
C dl – Capella de luxe
C std – Capella standard
Def – Defiant
Dove – Dove II
Peg – Pegasus
PII – Pegasus II
200 dl – 200 Capella de luxe
200 st – 200 Capella standard

Perky model with DKR Dove in 1957

DMW

	Engine	60	61	62	63	64	65	66	67	68	69	70
98 ts	6F	Bambi	Bambi									
197 ts	9E	Mk9	Mk9	Mk9	Mk9							
197 ts	9E				9/M	9/M						
197 ts	9E	12Tr										
197 ts	9E	12MX										
246 ts	32A	12Tr	12Tr	15Tr	17Tr	17Tr	17Tr					
246 ts	33A	12MX	12MX									
246 ts	34A			14MX								
246 ts	36A					14MX	19MX					
247 ts	Star				16MX	18MX	18MX					
247 ts	Star				Hor	Hor	Hor	Hor	Hor			
247 ts twin	Velo							Deem				
249 ts twin	2T	Dol	Dol	Dol	Dol		Dol					
249 ts twin	2T				DolM							
249 ts twin	4T					DolM						
249 ts twin	2T			DST	DST							
249 ts twin	2T				DSTM							
249 ts twin	4T					DSTM	DSTM	DSTM				
249 ts twin	2T	10Tr	10Tr									
249 ts twin	2T	10MX	10MX									
249 ts twin	2T		Deem	Deem	Deem							
249 ts twin	4T					Deem	Deem	Deem				
324 ts twin	3T	DolA	DolA	DolA								

Numbers refer to marks and M is a frame type. Tr indicates a trials model, and MX a scrambler.

Deem – Deemster
Dol – Dolomite
DST – Dolomite Sports Twin (See also the main text)
Hor – Hornet racer

Star – Starmaker
Velo – Velocette Viceroy engine

DOT

	Engine	60	61	62	63	64	65	66	67	68	69	70
197 ts	9E	SH										
197 ts	9E	SCH										
197 ts	9E	SDH										
197 ts	9E	THX										
197 ts	9E	TDHX										
197 ts	9E	WR	TM									
246 ts	33A	SH										
246 ts	33A	SDH										
246 ts	33A	SCH										
246 ts	34A		SCH	SCH								
246 ts	31A	THX										
246 ts	31A	TDHX										
246 ts	32A	WR	WR	WR	WR	WR	WR	WR				
246 ts	37A								S Tr	S Tr		
246 ts	32A		TM									
246 ts	32A/A				WRA	WRA	WRA	WRA	WRA	WRA		

Engine		60	61	62	63	64	65	66	67	68	69	70
246 ts	34A/M			Dem								
246 ts	36A				Dem	Dem	Dem					
246 ts	D/A						Dem	Dem	Dem	Dem		
246 ts	A		Cal									
247 ts	Star				Dem							
349 ts twin	RCA	SR										
349 ts twin	RCA	ST										
360 ts	D/A								Dem	Dem		

/A – alloy top half SR – Sportsman Roadster
Cal – Californian ST – SCH Twin WR
D/A – Dot/Alpha engine Star – Starmaker
Dem – Demon S Tr – Standard Trials
/M – Marcelle top half TM – Trials Marshall

EXCELSIOR

Engine		60	61	62	63	64	65	66	67	68	69	70
98 ts	6F	F10	F11	F12					Consort			
98 ts	6F	C10	C11		C14	C14			Consort			
98 ts	6F		EC11	EC12					Consort			
147 ts	Ex	MK1	K11	K12					Monarch			
147 ts	Ex	ME1	E11	E12					Monarch			
147 ts	Ex			U12					Courier			
148 ts	31C	U10	U11		U14	U14	U14		Universal			
197 ts	9E	R10	R11						Roadmaster			
197 ts	9E		E9						Golden V			
197 ts	9E		ER11									
243 ts twin	Ex	TT6	TT7						Talisman			
243 ts twin	Ex		ETT7	ETT8					Talisman			
328 ts twin	Ex	S9	S10	ETT9					Talisman			

Ex – Excelsior engine

Francis-Barnett Cruiser 84 with nice enclosure and nasty AMC engine

FRANCIS–BARNETT

	Engine	60	61	62	63	64	65	66	67	68	69	70
149 ts	AMC	86	86	86		95	95			Plover		
149 ts	AMC						96	96		Plover		
149 ts	AMC			88	88	88	88			Fulmar		
149 ts	AMC				90	90	90			Sports Fulmar		
171 ts	AMC	79								Light Cruiser		
199 ts	AMC	87	87	87	87	87	87	87		Falcon		
246 ts	32A				92	92	92	92		Trials		
246 ts	36A				93	93				Scrambles		
247 ts	Star					94	94	94				
249 ts	AMC	80	80	80	80					Cruiser		
249 ts	AMC	84	84	84						Cruiser		
249 ts	AMC	82	82	82						Scrambles		
249 ts	AMC	85	85	85						Trials		
249 ts twin	2T			89	89					Cruiser Twin		
249 ts twin	4T					89	89	89		Cruiser Twin		
249 ts twin	2T				91					Sports Cruiser		
249 ts twin	4T					91	91	91		Sports Cruiser		

Star – Starmaker

GREEVES

	Engine	60	61	62	63	64	65	66	67	68	69	70
197 ts	9E	20DB	20DC	20DC	20DC	20DC	20DC	20DC				
197 ts	9E	20SCS	20SCS	20SC								
197 ts	9E	20TC	20TD	20TD								
197 ts	9E	20TCS			20TE	20TE	20TE	20TE				
246 ts	32A	24DB	24DC	24DC								
246 ts	34A/G		24MCS	24MDS	24MDS	24MDS	24MDS					
246 ts	34A				24MD	24MD	24MD					
246 ts	Ch					24MX1	24MX2	24MX3	24MX5			
246 ts	Grif									24MX4	Grif	Grif
246 ts	36A/G				24RAS							
246 ts	Ch					24RBS	24RCS	24RDS	24RES	24RES		
246 ts	33A	24SCS	24SCS	24SC								
246 ts	32A	24TCS	24TDS	24TD								
246 ts	32A			24TE	24TE	24TE	24TE					
246 ts	32A/G			24TES	24TES	24TES	24TFS	24TGS				
246 ts	37A/Ch								24THS	24TJS		
246 ts	37A									24TJ		
246 ts	34A/G		ISDT	ISDT	ISDT							
247 ts	Star				24ME							
249 ts twin	2T	25DB	25DC	25DC	25DC	25DC						
249 ts twin	2T			25DCX	25DCX	25DCX						
249 ts twin	2T				25DD							
249 ts twin	4T					25DD	25DD					
249 ts twin	4T						25DC	25DC				
324 ts twin	3T	32DB	32DC	32DC	32DC	32DC						
324 ts twin	3T			32DCX	32DCX	32DCX						
324 ts twin	3T				32DD							
344 ts	Ch									35RFS		
362 ts	Ch								36MX4	36MX4		
380 ts	Grif										Grif	Grif

Ch – Challenger   /G – Greeves top half   Grif – Griffon   Star – Starmaker

HERCULES

	Engine	60	61	62	63	64	65	66	67	68	69	70
49 ts	HC5	Cor	Cor									

Cor – Corvette

JAMES

	Engine	60	61	62	63	64	65	66	67	68	69	70
98 ts	4F	L1	L1							Comet		
98 ts	6F	L1	L1	L1	L1	L1				Comet		
149 ts	AMC	L15A	L15A	L15A						Flying Cadet		
149 ts	AMC				M15	M15	M15			Cadet		
149 ts	AMC						M16	M16				
149 ts	AMC	SC1	SC1	SC1	SC4	SC4	SC4			Scooter		
199 ts	AMC	L20	L20	L20	L20	L20	L20	L20		Captain		
199 ts	AMC		L20S	L20S	L20S	L20S	L20S	L20S		Sports Captain		
246 ts	32A				M25T	M25T	M25T	M25T		Commando		
246 ts	36A/P				M25R	M25R				Cotswold		
247 ts	Star					M25RS	M25RS	M25RS		Cotswold		
249 ts	AMC	L25	L25	L25						Commodore		
249 ts	AMC	L25T	L25T	L25T						Commando		
249 ts	AMC	L25S	L25S	L25S						Cotswold		
249 ts twin	2T			M25	M25					Superswift		
249 ts twin	2T				M25S					Sports Superswift		
249 ts twin	4T					M25S	M25S	M25S		Sports Superswift		

/P – Parkinson top half
Star – Starmaker

Formidable Matchless G80CS scrambler that required real muscle when raced

NORMAN

	Engine	60	61	62	63	64	65	66	67	68	69	70
50 ts	Mi-Val	NIII	NIII									
50 ts	3K	NIV	NIV	NIV								
50 ts	Sachs	SL	SL									
50 ts	Mo			L								
50 ts	Mo			NV								
197 ts	9E	B2/S	B2/S									
197 ts	9E	B2/Sdl	B2/Sdl			Roadster						
197 ts	9E	B2/Sdl	B2/Sdl			Sports						
197 ts	9E	B2CS	B4C			Competition						
246 ts	32A		B4C			Trials						
246 ts	34A		B4C			Scrambles						
249 ts twin	2T	B/3	B4	B4		Roadster						
249 ts twin	2T	B/3	B4	B4		Sports						

L – Lido   Mo – Moto   N – Nippy   SL – Super Lido

NORTON

	b × s	60	61	62	63	64	65	66	67	68	69	70
249 ohv twin	60 × 44	Jub	Jub	Jub	Jub	Jub	Jub	Jub				
348 ohc	76 × 76.7	40M	40M	40M	40M							
348 ohv	71 × 88	50	50	50	50							
348 ohv	72 × 85.5					50	50	50				
349 ohv twin	63 × 56		Nav	Nav	Nav	Nav	Nav					
383 ohv twin	66 × 56				Ele	Ele	Ele					
490 ohv	79 × 100	ES2	ES2	ES2	ES2							
497 ohv	86 × 85.5					ES2	ES2	ES2				
497 ohc	86 × 85.62	30M	30M	30M	30M							
497 ohv twin	66 × 72.6	88	88	88	88							
497 ohv twin	66 × 72.6	88dl	88dl	88dl								
497 ohv twin	66 × 72.6	88No										
497 ohv twin	66 × 72.6		88SS	88SS	88SS	88SS	88SS	88SS				
596 ohv twin	68 × 82	99	99	99								
596 ohv twin	68 × 82	99dl	99dl	99dl								
596 ohv twin	68 × 82	99No										
596 ohv twin	68 × 82		99SS	99SS								
646 ohv twin	68 × 89		650	650	650							
646 ohv twin	68 × 89			650dl								
646 ohv twin	68 × 89			650SS	650SS	650SS	650SS	650SS	650SS	650SS	Mer	Mer
745 ohv twin	73 × 89			Atlas	Atlas	Atlas	Atlas	Atlas	Atlas	Atlas		
745 ohv twin	73 × 89				At MX	N	N	N	N15	N15CS		
745 ohv twin	73 × 89								P11	P11A		
745 ohv twin	73 × 89									20	20	
745 ohv twin	73 × 89										FB	FB
745 ohv twin	73 × 89										R	Ro
745 ohv twin	73 × 89										S	S

At MX – Atlas scrambler   Mer – Mercury   P11A – P11A, later Ranger
Ele – Electra   N – N15CSN   Ro – Roadster
FB – Fastback   Nav – Navigator
Jub – Jubilee   No – Nomad

Customized Norton Commando, by Paul Dunstall, beside
the Laxey Wheel in the Isle of Man

Dresda Triton in Putney, near Dave Degens' shop, where this nice machine was prepared in 1966. Pity about the rain

PANTHER

	Engine	60	61	62	63	64	65	66	67	68	69	70
174 ts	2L	173KS	173KS	173KS	173KS							
174 ts	2L	173ES	173ES	173ES								
197 ts	8E	10/3										
197 ts	9E	10/3A	10/3A	10/3A								
197 ts	9E	10/4	10/4	10/4								
197 ts	9E			197KS								
197 ts	9E			197ES								
249 ts twin	2T	35			35	35	35	35	35	35		
249 ts twin	2T	35Sp	35Sp	35Sp								
324 ts twin	3T	45	45	45	45	45						
324 ts twin	3T	50	50	50								
	b × s											
249 ohv	60 × 88	65										
348 ohv	71 × 88	75	75									
594 ohv	87 × 100	100	100	100	100							
645 ohv	88 × 106	120	120	120	120	120	120	120	120			

Sp – Sports

PHILLIPS

	Engine	60	61	62	63	64	65	66	67	68	69	70
50 ts	Rex	P40										
50 ts	Rex	P49	P49									
50 ts	Rex	P50	P50	P50								
50 ts	3K	P45	P45	P45								
50 ts	Mo			PM1	PM1	PM1						
50 ts	Mo			PM2	PM2	PM2						

Mo – Mobylette

PHOENIX

	Engine	60	61	62	63	64	65	66	67	68	69	70
98 ts	6F				100	100						
147 ts	30C	150	150	150								
148 ts	31C	150dl	150dl	150dl	150dl	150dl						
148 ts	31C	S150	S150	S150	S150	S150						
174 ts	2L	175	175	175	175	175						
174 ts	2L	175dl	175dl	175dl	175dl	175dl						
174 ts	2L	S175	S175	S175	S175	S175						
197 ts	9E	200	200	200	200	200						
197 ts	9E	200dl	200dl	200dl	200dl	200dl						
197 ts	9E	S200	S200	S200	S200	S200						
249 ts twin	2T	T250	T250	T250	T250	T250						
249 ts twin	2T				250dl	250dl						
324 ts twin	3T	T325	T325	T325	T325	T325						
324 ts twin	3T				325dl	325dl						

RALEIGH

	b × s	60	61	62	63	64	65	66	67	68	69	70
49.9 ts	38 × 44	RM2C										
49.8 ts	39 × 41.8		RM4	RM4	RM4							
49.8 ts	39 × 41.8		RM5	RM5	RM5	RM5	RM5	RM5	RM5	RM5	RM5	
49.8 ts	39 × 41.8			RM6	RM6	RM6	RM6	RM6	RM6	RM6	RM6	RM6
49.8 ts	39 × 41.8						RM6dl	RM6dl	RM6dl	RM6dl	RM6dl	
49.8 ts	39 × 41.8								RM6Pop			
49.8 ts	39 × 41.8								RM7	RM7	RM7	
49.8 ts	39 × 41.8					RM8	RM8	RM8	RM8	RM8	RM8	
49.8 ts	39 × 41.8					RM9	RM9	RM9	RM9	RM9	RM9	
49.8 ts	39 × 41.8								RM9/1	RM9/1	RM9/1	
49.8 ts	39 × 41.8							RM11	RM11			
49.8 ts	39 × 41.8						RM12	RM12	RM12			
78 ts	48 × 43		RS1	RS1								
78 ts	48 × 43			RS2	RS2	RS2						
78 ts	48 × 43					RS3						

ROYAL ENFIELD

	b × s	60	61	62	63	64	65	66	67	68	69	70
148 ts	56 × 60	Pr	Pr	Pr								
246 ts	66 × 72						GP5	GP5				
247 ts	68 × 68						Sc					
248 ohv	70 × 64.5	Cr	Cr	Cr								
248 ohv	70 × 64.5	Cl	Cl	Cl	Cl	Cl	Cl					
248 ohv	70 × 64.5	CrSp	CrSp	CrSp	CrSp	CrSp	CrSp	CrSp				
248 ohv	70 × 64.5			Su5	Su5		Ol					
248 ohv	70 × 64.5			Tr	Tr							
248 ohv	70 × 64.5				Cont	Cont	Cont					
248 ohv	70 × 64.5						GT	GT				
249 ts twin	50 × 63.5				TT	TT						
249 ts twin	50 × 63.5				TTS	TTS	TTS					
346 ohv	70 × 90	Bul	Bul	Bul								
346 ohv	70 × 90	Cl	Cl	Cl	NB	NB	NB					
346 ohv	70 × 90	WRT	WRT	WRT								
496 ohv twin	70 × 64.5	MM	MM	MM								
496 ohv twin	70 × 64.5	MMS	MMS	MMS	ST							
499 ohv	84 × 90	Bul	Bul	Bul								
693 ohv twin	70 × 90	SM	SM	SM								
693 ohv twin	70 × 90	Co	Co	Co	Co s/c							
736 ohv twin	71 × 93				Int	Int	Int			Int	Sell	Sell
736 ohv twin	71 × 93											Ri En

Bul – Bullet
Cl – Clipper
Co – Constellation
Cont – Continental
Co s/c – Constellation sidecar
Cr – Crusader
GT – Continental GT
Int – Interceptor

MM – Meteor Minor
MMS – Meteor Minor Sports
NB – New Bullet
Ol – Olympic
Pr – Prince
Ri En – Rickman Enfield
Sc – Scrambler
Sell – Series II

SM – Super Meteor
Sp – Sports
ST – Sports Twin
Su5 – Super 5
Tr – Trials
TT – Turbo Twin
TTS – Turbo Twin Sports
WRT – Works Replica Trials

1970 Rickman with the normal immaculate finish, front and rear disc brakes, and a screen

SCORPION

Engine		60	61	62	63	64	65	66	67	68	69	70
197 ts	9E				Tr							
246 ts	32A				Tr	Tr						
246 ts	GP5						GP5					
246 ts	36A				MX	MX	MX					
247 ts	Star				MX	MX	MX					

MX – Moto-cross Mk4
Star – Starmaker
Tr – Trials and Trials Mk2

SCOTT

	b × s	60	61	62	63	64	65	66	67	68	69	70
345 ts twin	60.2 × 60.2						Racer	Racer	Racer			
497 ts twin	66.6 × 71.4	FS	FS	FS	FS	FS	FS	FS	FS	FS	FS	FS
598 ts twin	73 × 71.4	FS	FS	FS	FS	FS	FS	FS	FS	FS	FS	FS

FS – Flying Squirrel

SPRITE

Engine		60	61	62	63	64	65	66	67	68	69	70
125 ts	Sachs										Tr	Tr
246 ts	32A					Tr	Tr	Tr	Tr			
246 ts	Al/Gr					Sc	Sc	Sc	Sc			
247 ts	Star							Mo Tr	Mo Tr			
247 ts	Star							Mo Sc	Mo Sc			
247 ts	Sp											250MX
360 ts	Sp									Sp 360		
399 ts	Sp										405MX	405MX
500 Frame	—					kit	kit	kit				

Al/Gr – Alpha and Greeves engine   Sc – Scrambles
Mo Sc – Monza scrambler   Sp – Sprite
Mo Tr – Monza trials   Star – Starmaker
MX – Moto-cross   Tr – Trials

SUN

Engine		60	61	62	63	64	65	66	67	68	69	70
98 ts	6F	Geni										
174 ts	2L	S	SII									
174 ts	2L		KS									

KS – Sunwasp KS
S – Sunwasp
SII – Sunwasp MkII

SUNBEAM

	b × s	60	61	62	63	64	65	66	67	68	69	70
172 ts	61.5 × 58	B1	B1	B1	B1	B1	B1					
249 ohv twin	56 × 50.6	B2	B2	B2	B2	B2						
249 ohv twin	56 × 50.6	B2S	B2S	B2S	B2S	B2S						

TRIUMPH

	b × s	60	61	62	63	64	65	66	67	68	69	70
100 ts	50.4 × 50			Tina	Tina	Tina	Tina					
100 ts	50.4 × 50						T10	T10	T10	T10	T10	T10
172 ts	61.5 × 58	TS1	TS1	TS1	TS1	TS1	TS1					
199 ohv	63 × 64	T20	T20	T20	T20	T20	T20	T20	T20SC	T20SC		
199 ohv	63 × 64	T20S	T20T									
199 ohv	63 × 64		T20S/L	T20S/H	T20S/H	T20S/H	T20S/H	T20S/H				
199 ohv	63 × 64		T20S/S	T20S/S	T20S/S	T20S/S	T20S/S	T20S/S				
199 ohv	63 × 64			TS20	TS20	TS20						
199 ohv	63 × 64			TR20	TR20	TR20	TR20	TR20				
199 ohv	63 × 64						T20SM	T20SM				
247 ohv	67 × 70									TR25W	TR25W	TR25W
249 ohv twin	56 × 50.6	TW2	TW2	TW2	TW2	TW2						
249 ohv twin	56 × 50.6	TW2S	TW2S	TW2S	TW2S	TW2S						
349 ohv twin	58.2 × 65.5	3TA	3TA	3TA	3TA	3TA	3TA	3TA				
349 ohv twin	58.2 × 65.5				T90	T90	T90	T90	T90	T90	T90	
490 ohv twin	69 × 65.5	5TA	5TA	5TA	5TA	5TA	5TA	5TA				
490 ohv twin	69 × 65.5	T100A	T100A					T100				
490 ohv twin	69 × 65.5		T100SS	T100SS	T100SS	T100SS	T100SS	T100C	T100C	T100C	T100C	
490 ohv twin	69 × 65.5							T100R	T100R	T100R	T100R	
490 ohv twin	69 × 65.5								T100S	T100S	T100S	T100S
490 ohv twin	69 × 65.5								T100T	T100T	T100T	T100T
649 ohv twin	71 × 82	6T	6T	6T	6T	6T	6T	6T				
649 ohv twin	71 × 82	T110	T110									
649 ohv twin	71 × 82	T120	T120	T120	T120	T120	T120	T120	T120	T120	T120	T120
649 ohv twin	71 × 82						T120Th	T120R	T120R			
649 ohv twin	71 × 82							T120TT	T120TT			
649 ohv twin	71 × 82	TR6	TR6	TR6	TR6	TR6	TR6	TR6	TR6	TR6	TR6	TR6
649 ohv twin	71 × 82							TR6C	TR6C			
649 ohv twin	71 × 82							TR6R	TR6R			
740 ohv triple	67 × 70										T150	T150

T120Th – Thruxton Bonneville

VELOCETTE

	b × s	60	61	62	63	64	65	66	67	68	69	70
192 sv twin	50 × 49	LE	LE	LE	LE	LE	LE	LE	LE	LE	LE	LE
192 sv twin	50 × 49				Vo	Vo	Vo	Vo	Vo	Vo		
192 ohv twin	50 × 49	Va	Va	Va	Va	Va						
192 ohv twin	50 × 49	VaVe										
247 ts twin	54 × 54		Vic	Vic	Vic	Vic						
349 ohv	68 × 96	MAC										
350 ohv	72 × 86	Vi	Vi	Vi	Vi	Vi	Vi	Vi	Vi			
350 ohv	72 × 86		Vi Ve	Vi Ve	Vi Ve	Vi Ve	Vi Ve	Vi Ve	Vi Ve	Vi Ve		
350 ohv	72 × 86	Sc	Sc	Sc	Sc	Sc	Sc	Sc	Sc	Sc		
350 ohv	72 × 86				Vi Sp	Vi Sp	Vi Sp	Vi Sp	Vi Sp	Vi Sp		
499 ohv	86 × 86	MSS	MSS	MSS	MSS	MSS	MSS	MSS	MSS	MSS	MSS	MSS
499 ohv	86 × 86	M Sc	M Sc	M Sc	M Sc	M Sc	M Sc	M Sc	M Sc	M Sc		
499 ohv	86 × 86	Ven	Ven	Ven	Ven	Ven	Ven	Ven	Ven	Ven	Ven	Ven
499 ohv	86 × 86		Ven Ve	Ven Ve	Ven Ve	Ven Ve	Ven Ve	Ven Ve	Ven Ve	Ven Ve	Ven Ve	Ven Ve
499 ohv	86 × 86				Ven Sp	Ven Sp	Ven Sp	Ven Sp	Ven Sp	Ven Sp		
499 ohv	86 × 86	En	En	En	En	En	En	En	En	En	En	
499 ohv	86 × 86						Thr	Thr	Thr	Thr	Thr	Thr

En – Endurance
M Sc – MSS scrambler
Sc – Scrambler
Thr – Thruxton
Va – Valiant
Ve – Veeline
Ven – Venom and Venom Clubman

Ven Ve – Venom and Venom Clubman Veeline
Ven Sp – Venom Special
Vi – Viper and Viper Clubman
Vi Ve – Viper and Viper Clubman Veeline
Vi Sp – Viper Special
Vic – Viceroy
Vo – Vogue

Velocette single having its tick-over adjusted, and representing tradition

In contrast was the Ariel Leader, with its two-stroke twin engine and full enclosure. This one has a 1974 number

Blackpool Winter Gardens staged a small, but good show in May 1963, when Honda were up in the balcony and the only Japanese firm attending

Acknowledgements

This book was written as part of a larger-format series in the Osprey Collector's Library and, for me, differed from *British Motorcycles of the 1930s*. That was about the tired machines which I rode in my youth, while this one covers a very different era. It was a period I lived through, of course, beginning with racing, going on to organize road-race meetings, and starting a writing career. In those days, writing was very much a part-time, leisure activity; now it occupies me full time, and leaves little to spare.

Thanks for help with this book go mainly to those who helped with the pictures and, once more, I am indebted to EMAP, whose archives hold the old *Motor Cycle Weekly* files. Other photos came from the *Motor Cycle News* files, courtesy of editor Malcolm Gough, and some were provided by Nick Nicholls from his extensive collection.

This is the first in the series to have a colour section, the plates for which also came from the EMAP archives and are of machines that have been featured in *Classic Bike* in recent years. My thanks to Mike Nicks, editor of that magazine, for kindly writing the foreword to this work.

A number of pictures carried the imprints of professionals, and photos used came from Atlas Studios, Cecil Bailey, Richard Bailey, Billy Bleach, Boswell Barratt and Phillips, Brooks Photographers, Reg Cave, Court Studio, Edgar Hopkinson, Industrial Photographic, H. E. Jones, Kingston Photographic Supply, Donald Page, Phillips Cycles, Photowork, Publifoto, Rimmer Industrial Photography, F. B. Scott, Sport & General, Tidbury Studios, Thomas Wilkie and Woburn Studios. As usual, all the pictures were returned to their files after publication, and I have tried to make contact to clear copyright. If my letter failed to reach you, or I have used an unmarked print without realizing this, please accept my apologies.

Finally, my thanks to Tony Thacker, my editor, and all the Osprey production team for their help and assistance.

Roy Bacon
Niton, Isle of Wight
December 1987

Dennis Poore talking to Freddie Frith, seated on a Norton Commando, in 1968. Poore was much involved with the demise of the industry, Frith simply one of the road-racing greats

<u>NOTES</u>

<u>NOTES</u>